An Ene...
Book ... Dying

An Energy Healer's Book of Dying

For Caregivers and Those in Transition

SUZANNE WORTHLEY

FINDHORN PRESS

Findhorn Press
One Park Street
Rochester, Vermont 05767
www.findhornpress.com

SUSTAINABLE FORESTRY INITIATIVE

Certified Sourcing
www.sfiprogram.org
SFI-00854

Text stock is SFI certified

Findhorn Press is a division of Inner Traditions International

Disclaimer

The information in this book is given in good faith and intended for information only. Neither author nor publisher can be held liable by any person for any loss or damage whatsoever which may arise from the use of this book or any of the information therein.

Cataloging-in-Publication data for this title is available from the Library of Congress

ISBN 978-1-64411-032-4 (print)
ISBN 978-1-64411-033-1 (ebook)

Printed and bound in the United States by Lake Book Manufacturing, Inc. The text stock is SFI certified. The Sustainable Forestry Initiative® program promotes sustainable forest management.

10 9 8 7 6 5 4 3 2 1

Edited by Michael Hawkins
Cover illustration by Kay Pat
Text design, layout and illustrations by Damian Keenan
This book was typeset in Adobe Garamond Pro and Museo Sans with
Old Claude LP used as a display typeface.

To send correspondence to the author of this book, mail a first-class letter to the author c/o Inner Traditions • Bear & Company, One Park Street, Rochester, VT 05767, USA and we will forward the communication, or contact the author directly at **www.sworthley.com**

Dedication

I dedicate this book to *anyone* who is experiencing the death process in *any manner*, whether it is someone in the midst of their own personal journey, a family member or friend assisting a loved one, a volunteer offering their time and service, or a medical staff member whose life work is to help others in this grand transformation of energy.

The process of death, of returning to spirit, is one of the most personal and sacred transitions we will experience in our lifetime. With this book, I will do my best to honor just that. I offer the concepts in this guide as possibilities to ponder and the ideas as an expansion of current beliefs.

My goal in writing this book is to present, from my perspective as a psychic and energy healer, an expanded vision or understanding of what is happening *energetically* during each stage of the death process. In doing so, I hope to counter any fear or angst normally associated with the process of death and bring solace, awareness, and empowerment to those experiencing or witnessing a return to spirit.

I ultimately dedicate this book to all of those celestial souls in transition, making their own personal journey back home. May their experience be one of wonder and joy.

Contents

PART III: Rituals and Goodbyes

Appendices

Introduction

I grew up as the daughter of a mortician. As a child, I never thought of my father's job as different or odd. Actually, I never really thought about it at all. My mother stayed home to raise my five siblings and me, while my father spent his days working in the funeral home. For some, a funeral home can be an uncomfortable place, but for me, it was a second home. I spent every Saturday there after piano lessons. It was my father's office. It was where we hung out. It was a normal part of life—just like riding in the hearse. For some, a hearse represents dread and sorrow, but for me it was our family car, which could easily tote around six children.

Later on, I learned my upbringing wasn't all that conventional. Most kids didn't talk about death and dying at the dinner table alongside the usual topics of school, grades, and boyfriends. It wasn't until high school when I noticed a difference in the way my friends thought about death. I admit I could cause quite a stir in a group of teenagers when they found out I was a mortician's daughter. Even today, I still find most folks are uncomfortable with the subject of dying. I personally never thought of death as something scary, icky, or weird. I certainly didn't perceive my father working with death as something scary, icky, or weird. I believed then (and now) that death is simply part of our life path. It is not to be feared as much as embraced. Even as a child, I intuitively knew that any professional who assisted the loved ones left behind during their loved one's journey of "going home" must be a person with a *gift*. My father has that gift, and he chose to share it with others. I found my own version of this gift.

As an energy practitioner, spiritual healer, and hospice volunteer, I have had the opportunity to use this gift and spend numerous hours with people during what I feel is one of the most profound energetic and spiritual experiences ever—*their death*. I have witnessed first-hand, through the use of my psychic abilities and knowledge of our human energy systems, their incredible journey back to spirit. My hospice patients are so loving and giving of themselves. They are my teachers. Their homes and hospital rooms are my classrooms. I'm blessed they allow me to share such a personal, spiritual time and space, and I feel it is time to finally share what I have learned to help people through their own personal journey, whether they are the patient, the family member, the loved one, the friend, or the medical staff.

Doing this work has allowed me to find a unique perspective on how the soul processes and works in energy. I want to share first-hand what I *see* and offer you a new way to look at death using *psychic sight*. When we look at death only with our human eyes, we are often consumed by fear and sadness. But when we understand how to use *psychic sight*, we can move through the process in love and spirit. There are many who do not necessarily view the process of death as a gift, and I understand that this can be a hard concept to embrace. *That is why I wrote this book: to replace fear with knowledge. To encourage willing participation. To give power back to those who own it. To affirm miracles. To help people see through the perspective of the heart rather than the limited perspective of the ego.*

This book is divided into three parts. In the first, I give some helpful background information: a description of how life-force energy works, what the Akashic records and soul contracts are, and an overview of the energetic stages of the death process. In the second part, we'll go step-by-step through the nine energetic levels of dying, so you can understand what is happening at each level, know what to watch for in each stage, and learn specific ways in which you can support your loved one through their transition back to spirit. Additionally, I have included actual hospice visits as case studies so that you can see how others have experienced the stages of death in various ways. These case studies examine, on an energetic level, the experiences some hospice patients have had while shutting down specific chakras. I share these to assist you in seeing how energy blocks can affect the death process and understanding how clearing old beliefs while living can directly affect the way we die.

In the third part I offer a simple farewell ritual as well as some insight into the grieving process and helpful strategies for moving through it. Additionally you will find two appendices: The first appendix features one additional case study and other death experiences. The second appendix presents the most important and helpful information on the nine transition stages and healing strategies in an easily accessible "at-a-glance" format.

You do not have to be psychic to have experiences similar to those you will read on the pages ahead. Anyone who has assisted a loved one, friend, or patient through the death process has most likely come into contact with some, or all, of the phases involved. Without the knowledge of what they are experiencing, the events are often dismissed or downplayed. Many find themselves doubting what they actually saw or felt as they walked with a loved one through the death process. The feelings in the room. The sensation of spiritual visitors. The shifting movement of light. The *coincidences* of how things and timing played out. By learning the phases of the journey to spirit, we can embrace the stages in a new light—one of divine energy.

Just like my father used his gift to help families through the funeral process, my purpose is to offer perspectives to help the dying person and his or her family members and friends move through the energetic death process. I do not in any way mean to impose my vision on others. Death is personal, private, and probably one of the more sacred occurrences we encounter, either for our self or our loved ones. I only offer my perspective as a gift of sharing. But before we can examine the death process, we must first understand life—the energy that not only creates the human form, but also fuels and maintains it while we're living.

A Note on Unexpected Deaths

This book presents what is happening on an energetic level when the death occurs as a natural process rather than as a sudden, accidental, or violent event. It also outlines the progression of the levels of transition in a numerical sequence that may or may not happen in order, meaning many people jump from one level to another, sometimes revisiting levels until full transition is complete.

Unexpected (usually sudden) deaths have an energy signature that is significantly different from the natural dying process covered in this book. I plan to address unexpected deaths in a different book, but you can utilize the Akashic Record information presented in the Akashic Record and Soul Contracts chapter as insight for possible how's and why's of a difficult passing.

If you have lost a loved one unexpectedly or tragically, one of the best ways to help is by allowing yourself to trust there is love and assistance available to the person during the death process in terms of guides, angels, guardians, and deceased loved ones all there to support the crossing. Holding the energy of this belief on behalf of the recently deceased gives strength to the process happening on the spiritual plane, while offering you a step toward healing yourself on the physical plane. Ways to hold energy can include prayer, meditation, celebration, ritual, or just about anything your heart desires to create. This effort does not need to be maintained nor end at any significant time or date. In fact, many people enjoy marking noteworthy dates of their deceased loved ones like holidays or birthdays as a time to celebrate and further assist in the overall healing process.

Other things you can do to provide support and assistance from the physical side of life include:

- Communicate with your loved one, out loud or in your heart, and don't worry about getting "an answer."
- Continue to send love for their ongoing transition.
- Make peace within your own heart, mind, and body by honoring their choice to move back to Source.

- Stay in touch with others who may have been affected by the loss, to assist them in their grief process, as well as your own.
- Do your best to find joy in moving forward, while honoring your individual personal timing for grieving and loss.

PART I

Life-Force Energy and the Death Process

Life-Force Energy

As humans, everything we do requires energy. We need energy each morning to open our eyes, get out of bed, and plan what we'll do next. From our first month in the womb to our ending days, our bodies use this energy to keep life flowing. You can think of this energy like fuel and your body the vehicle.

So what is this fuel and where does it come from? It is a universal energy that flows through everything. It has no tangible form. Instead, it is energy from the same source that creates our cosmos, our Earth, and our human bodies. Many religions and belief systems have different ways to talk about this energy. Some call it God or the I AM. To simplify terms, I am going to call it Source, Source energy, or life-force.

Most of us don't spend much time thinking about Source energy and how it affects our daily lives. But we actually work with Source energy to create our human form in a process I call *co-creation*. If we can understand how Source energy flows into and sustains our body, we have more control over how we use this force. As beings who can co-create, we have the opportunity to work with Source in ways that enrich our lives and, when the day comes, also enrich our deaths.

To understand how we work with Source energy to co-create our lives, let's start by exploring the fundamental building blocks of how this life-force interacts with our physical bodies through three central structures called the *dimensions of light,* the *chakra system,* and the *aura.* Each structure represents a different aspect of our consciousness that is essential for living our lives and experiencing death. We'll define and explore each of these systems in the pages to come.

The First Structure: Dimensions of Light

When explaining the journey of co-creation to my clients, I typically start with the analogy of a layer cake. Everything exists within a giant layer-cake of energy: layers and layers, one on top of the other, that start at the bottom, beginning with the first layer, and move upward to the infinite. There is also no value system attached to these numbers and layers; higher is not "better." Each layer is simply a different layer of energy or light with its own vibration, density, and information. As a whole, this layer cake encompasses everything from the busy world around us, to the universe, to our individual bodies.

We experience Earth as humans in the third dimension—linear time, space, height, width, and length. The third dimension is near the bottom of the layer cake (third from the bottom). Most of us don't think much beyond this third-dimensional existence on a day-by-day basis. That isn't good or bad, right or wrong, it just is. For most of us, our connection to the human experience really only involves knowing the first three layers: the planet Earth (first layer or first dimension), plants and animals (second layer or second dimension), and the human form (third layer or third dimension).

Unless we find ways of connecting to higher dimensions (layer four and beyond) we pretty much exist in the third-dimensional world alone. I believe this is part of the reason why we're here: to allow Source energy to experience Earth in the third dimension. But as co-creators with Source, we have the opportunity to extend our understanding beyond the third dimension and recognize:

- We all come from Source and will return to Source.
- Our bodies are vehicles for Source energy in the third dimension.
- Source energy allows us to access other dimensions and be multi-dimensional.
- Each dimension of light contains information we can use to enrich our lives.
- When we access these higher dimensions, we can activate new levels of consciousness.

The dimensions of light are all about knowledge. Information is stored in each dimension and our consciousness can help us rediscover and use this information in our daily lives as well as during the time of our deaths.

Consciousness is the state of being aware of something within oneself. It has been defined as a sentience, awareness, having control over one's own mind, or having a sense of selfhood. To me, consciousness is being fully aware of my role and my own power in creating my life. It means trying my best to wrap my head and heart around the concept that I am manifesting or co-creating everything in my existence—good, bad, and ugly—each and every moment of my days. It's as if my life were a self-contained play in which I am not only the writer, the producer, the stage hands, and the actors, but also the audience.

Living fully connected to the responsibility of co-creation and being conscious of our every moment is a lot to comprehend and accept. I find many folks are more comfortable pondering the subject than actually embodying or manifesting it, while many choose to remain ignorant of or even reject the concept completely.

Oftentimes in the classes I teach, I ask for a show of hands of those who have had a conversation about consciousness in the last several days. The expression on the faces in the audience is priceless...confused, blank, eyes cast downward. Then I ask how many have had a conversation about their partner, their kids, their job, their new shoes? Every hand goes up and I have to explain that you cannot experience the partner, the kids, the job, or the shoes without you co-creating it in your consciousness, right?!?

Consciousness is a foundational essence of how we choose to live our existence. It is the ability to be aware and understand that although *we are living in the third dimension, we can access other dimensions of light that can help us move more peacefully through life and death.*

21

Summary

There indeed may be hundreds of layers of existence or dimensions of light, and we are each a part of every layer in all time, place, and space. This is hard to understand when we live in our human form in the third dimension. But because we contain life-force energy, we are part of the entire layer cake with Source being the frosting!

We are all vehicles for Source energy in the third dimension, and because of this Source energy, we have the ability to connect spiritually and energetically to access *infinite knowledge via the dimensions of light*. This infinite knowing is a part of our birthright, but as humans, we often forget most of what we know until we activate our higher senses and spiritually connect beyond the third dimension.

When we learn how to tap into these higher layers, we become aware of other bodies of co-creation. Just as we are the bodies of the third dimension, each layer has its own inhabitants, including those who serve as gatekeepers and helpers. Some of these are known as angels, arch-angels, master guides and teachers, and much more. When we are connected to these realms, we can find great solace in assistance from these gatekeepers not only in our lives, but also in our deaths. The *Human Being* is "supposed to be" the gatekeeper of the third dimension, on task for connecting collective humanity with the planet and its second-dimensional keepers of plants and animals. Personally, I am not impressed with how the collective human race is doing with this task of *gatekeeping the planet and its inhabitants*. If we understood our role in this bigger picture, I assume we would treat others with love and kindness, as well as take better care of our planet and its elemental kingdom.

The Second Structure: The Chakra System

The second structure vital for our life-force energy to function within the body is called the chakra system. "Chakra" is a Sanskrit word, and it means *wheel of energy*. The job of the chakra system is to push life-force energy throughout the human body and spirit. The system includes seven wheel-like spinning vortexes or energy centers that run down the center of the human body. Each chakra wheel corresponds to a layer or dimension of light coming from Source, as we explored earlier. You can think of the chakras as divine fueling destination points allowing cosmic "gas" to fuel your vehicle. They are not anatomical (not a physical part of your body), they are incredible energy centers that activate and ignite during gestation and de-activate during the death process. Because the human body is a vehicle of consciousness itself, the chakras fuel our human organs and our mental and emotional states as well as our spirit.

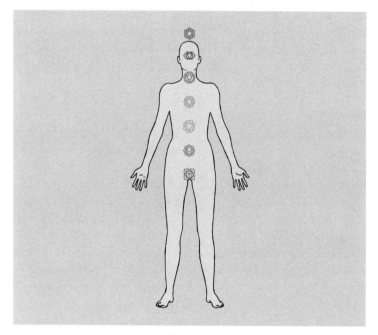

The Chakra System

Each chakra has its own job in fueling the body, and when they run at optimum levels, the human body is healthy, happy, and balanced. But when any chakra is not being fueled or is out of alignment with the Source, the body will be affected on a physical, emotional mental, or spiritual level. This dis-connect, or *dis-ease,* is what manifests as *"disease"* throughout the human experience. The human body energetically suffers or dies according to the imbalance of the life-force energy. In death, how the chakras shut down plays a key role in helping the human body return to spirit. We *de*-activate, the reverse of the birth activation, to die and return to Source.

I believe we choose to come here as an individual intention with a particular purpose and we have the privilege to *co-create through this chakra system.* When we understand the concept of our body as a vehicle (with the chakras as the system that brings in the fuel to run or power the vehicle), we can understand how important it is for us to maintain and fill our own tank, and begin to take more personal responsibility for our lives and our deaths. We can also better honor other's choices on how they find their fuel to run their own vehicle.

Summary

The second structure, the chakra system, moves life-force gas into our body directly from Source. When our chakras are running well, our energy is balanced and our body is healthy. When our chakras are out of alignment, we can become dis-eased.

Again, it is important to remember that dimensions of light allow us to access *all we know* from Source. Our individual bodies contain information in our DNA, our cells, and our energy bodies. Our meat-and-bone body holds most of our answers about our life as well as our death. Learning what we need to know, working with that information, and releasing what is no longer valid all happens via the chakra system. The foundational energy of *all we know in the dimensions of light* now begins to emerge as *all we create in the chakra system.*

The Third Structure: The Aura or Energy Body

Think of what it feels like the moment you first meet someone. You might innately sense you will get along well with this person. Or maybe you sense you will have trouble finding common ground.

Oftentimes, you perceive these feelings even before any words are spoken. This is because you're already picking up information energetically about who they are by sensing their aura.

The third structure for experiencing life-force energy is called the aura or energy body, which is a luminous body of energy that surrounds and interpenetrates our physical body. It is a structure that helps anchor the life-force energy to our physical body by taking the energy that comes in through the chakras and storing it in different layers called energy bodies or fields. Think of it like a gas tank. Each auric field stores the fuel being taken in by an individual chakra.

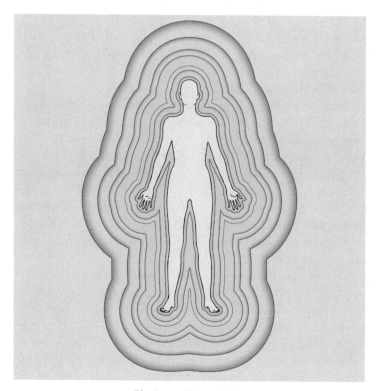

The Aura or Energy Body

These fields, or fuel tanks, hold Source energy and vibrate at their own frequency. If the chakras take in the fuel, the aura *allows us to embody Source energy.* It is this vibration we feel when we meet someone for the first time or can sense someone is near.

Summary

The third energy structure is called the aura and it primarily anchors life-force energy to our physical bodies. Source energy comes in through each chakra and moves to the aura where it is held or stored in its corresponding field. *All we experience or EMBODY moves through the aura.*

Life-Force Energy Summary

Again, you can think of the first structure, your conscious body accessing dimensions of light, as your vehicle for Source energy. The second structure, the chakras, take in the gas and use it to create power. The third structure, the aura, holds fuel like a gas tank. Not unlike an automobile, you need a vehicle that runs, gas to run it, and a tank to store the gas. When your vehicle is running in top shape, from good gas held via a healthy container, life is easy, synchronistic, and in harmony. If you have no gas, or a faulty tank, the vehicle will eventually break down and die. Our three foundational structures need to work in harmony. When we find dis-*ease* in any structure, we ultimately will find *disease* in our experience, whether it is physical, emotional, mental, or spiritual. This process is how the human form ultimately chooses to leave this 3-D plane of existence, and physically die.

Yes, I believe we do *choose to die.* This is a difficult concept for many when they, or their loved ones, are in the death experience. We do not necessarily see this as our choice in this plane of existence, but we do choose—from the soul's standpoint. Each of us, prior to our incarnation, co-creates our own Book of Life or our record of the embodiment we are entering into as a human existence. This record of the incoming life includes details that will be played out not only in life, but in death.

Akashic Records
and Soul Contracts

I magine you're out for a walk in the woods, and as you make your way through the trees, you happen upon an ancient structure. It's an old stone building with impressive carvings and columns covered in vines. Making your way around, you find stone steps that lead to a wooden door. The door is unlocked. You step inside, and once your eyes adjust, you realize you're in an expansive hall that seems to stretch on forever. The hall is lined with shelves holding billions of books, all different sizes and colors. But there is one book not on the shelf. Instead, this book is sitting open on a podium under a soft light. You approach the book, and as you turn the pages, you realize it's a recording of your life. It tells of your past as well as all possible futures you might encounter, leaving some pages empty for the choices you have yet to make. You have arrived at the Akashic Records.

Akashic Records

The Akashic Records, or "The Book of Life," has been studied by many for centuries. Most scholars agree it is some sort of record or embodiment of all that is and all that is possible in every form of energy and spirit. Christian mystic philosopher and intuitive healer Edgar Cayce recorded numerous readings and findings on the Akashic Records that to this day stand the test of time. The following is an excerpt from Edgar Cayce's Association for Research and Enlightenment on the Book of Life:

The Akashic Records...can be equated to the universe's supercomputer system. It is this system that acts as the central storehouse of all information for every individual who has ever lived upon earth.

More than just a reservoir of events, the Akashic Records contain every deed, word, feeling, thought, and intent that has ever occurred at any time in the history of the world. Much more than simply a memory storehouse, however, these Akashic Records are interactive in that they have a tremendous influence upon our everyday lives, our relationships, our feelings and belief systems, and the potential realities we draw toward us.

The Edgar Cayce readings suggest that from a soul standpoint, each of us co-creates our story, our Book of Life. For me, the Book includes the information about why we are here. It is the ability to actually *create the experience* that becomes manifest as our human life journey. Cayce references a central storehouse of all information for every individual who has ever lived upon the Earth. This storehouse is the Akashic Record. Each individual has their own book, or energetic file, of potentials and life possibilities. This file is interactive as long as the life path is still being played out, using the energies of free will and choice in re-editing the book's content. Unlike the visual of the great hall, the Akashic Records is not actually a physical building or library. Instead, these records are encoded in our bodies. We most likely store this information within our DNA, which contains our own unique genetic instruction, our genetic code or set of blueprints. The encoded energy remains interactive and continues to be adjusted by our thoughts, deeds, and free will actions. As we discussed in the previous chapter, we have the opportunity to partner with Source to shape our lives.

Our Akashic Record is constantly adjusted through choices and consequences being played out in our life experience. Some consider this constant adjustment as spiritual purification—cleansing, atonement, prayer, meditation, or forgiveness. Some see it as free will and choice. I often find clients and patients moving through the death process actively participating in this purification process. Consciously or unconsciously they are moving and transferring the energies of their file or Book of Life by realigning their thoughts, words, and deeds. Releasing old anger. Atoning for actions. Finding peace. Sometimes those of us in their presence can witness this. Other times we cannot, as it is done energetically and telepathically. Our records, the energetic files of our life, remain interactive until we return to Source through the completion of the human death experience. Then and only then is the Akashic Record a final and sealed energetic file held for eternity. In a sense, it is filed away and shelved in the great hall.

For the purpose of the death process, one of the most important elements of the Akashic Record is the date, time, place, and source of the person's human dying experience. If we believe that the elements of the process of a person's death are all part of their soul contract, then we can open our minds and hearts to the belief that the person indeed is in control of the elements of their journey from a higher plane in their existence. When we truly embrace this concept, we can begin to allow our loved one the opportunity to fulfill their soul contract in the manner they have originally planned prior to their birth and manifestation itself.

Soul Contract

So what is a soul contract? It is an agreement you make first and foremost with your celestial soul as to what you plan on accomplishing in this life. Your contract is developed prior to you incarnating as a being on Earth and is designed and created in consciousness with your God-Self or Higher Self. The elements of this contract reside in the Akashic Record which you carry within your divine mind and your energy bodies.

We make soul contracts with others—our parents, siblings, lovers, spouses, children, friends, and even enemies. Every person on the divine plane is a great ally and helper, though they may take more difficult roles in this third-dimensional lifetime as we experience challenges in the flesh. Even those that harm us are said to have a contract with us, and in the end, all of it is done in love. Our soul's reason for being is not only to fulfill our original divine plan, but also to balance our karmic debt. Our soul, seeking resolution, is compelled to revisit past karmic encounters lifetime after lifetime until we find that resolution.

In the beginning, our celestial soul decided and then chose to come into this incarnation. It was endowed with a unique and precious gift that is meant to be shared with others as a human co-creation. Through the process of the individual incarnation on Earth, we are also meant to evolve spiritually in life as well as in death.

Our celestial soul knows that when we have fulfilled our reason for being, we will joyfully return to realms of spirit to continue our soul's adventure. Most of us see death as an end, when actually, it is a transition of consciousness. Those who allow themselves or their loved ones to *go home* truly respect and honor the soul contract of the dying person. Fully understanding that the person dying knows from the celestial soul perspective that it is their time to go, and that they are following their own soul's timeline which is critical to their life's plan. Their soul contract chose the time, date, place, and situation of their death. The contract also chose who participates and how—meaning whether you are in attendance (or *not* in attendance) with a loved one for their death. Attendance is determined in the contract according to whatever each of us needs to experience.

When we allow ourselves to have a new understanding of co-creation and soul plans, we can open our minds and hearts to understand that death does not really exist. We will know that our opportunity to learn and to grow is never over and will continue on the other side of the veil. We can also release old programmed fears of the concept that we will either be rewarded or punished for how we lived our lives; this will never come when we understand co-creation because life is not about reward and punishment. That concept is old dogma perpetuated by fear.

We can also release the idea that there is a place we may or may not go to after death. Instead, we can recognize that death is transformation back to omnipresence. Life, as well as death, is a process of continuous and unending growth for not only our body, but ultimately for our soul—an expansion of self-expression, co-creation, and embodiment of all experiences. Explore the concept that death is simply a transition of your Source energy made manifest—a glorious movement forward to create the next experience of the soul. Death is an upgrade of knowledge, increasing our level of consciousness, a freedom-giving, pain-releasing, eternally transforming process of evolution.

Honor the soul contract of your loved one during their time of transition. Allowing a loved one the energetic space to go home in the manner they are creating is true unconditional love. Removing our personal ego from their death process is a critical element to making this transition smoother. One of the ways we can do this is to *let them die*, releasing us and them emotionally. We get to die. We get to return to Source. Giving them permission out loud or in your heart is important not only for them, but for you as well. Sometimes it is allowing them to die without our presence. If this happens, we need to release any guilt about not being at bedside as that may be the plan our loved one ultimately chose to play out. Again, honor their plan, honor their soul contract of how they chose to die. Offering prayers of release back to spirit is essential to their transition rather than holding onto that loved one in egotistical energetic terms fueling our own wants and needs.

And remember, if you are intimately involved with the life and death of a loved one, that means you most likely had a *soul contract* with them.

If we can honor the Higher Self-knowledge of the soul contract, we can assist in a loving journey, not escalate a fear-filled one. One result of this philosophy: many humans will know that death is not something to be feared, but a magical part of the glorious experience called Life itself. They will be able to experience the miracle of the death process outlined in the next pages.

Summary

As we discussed in the Life-Force Energy chapter, we have the opportunity to partner with Source to shape our lives. From a soul standpoint, each of us co-creates our story, our Book of Life or our

Akashic Record, which includes the information about why we are here. It is the instruction-set on how to actually *create the experience* that becomes manifest as our human life journey, and is constantly being adjusted through choices and consequences being played out in our life experience.

Your *soul contract* is an agreement you make with others—parents, siblings, lovers, spouses, children, friends, and even enemies—and includes elements of what you plan on accomplishing in this life. Your contract is developed prior to you incarnating as a being on Earth and is designed and created in consciousness with your God-Self or Higher Self. The elements of this contract reside in the Akashic Record, which you carry within your divine mind and your energy bodies. The Record is sealed as the final recording of the life-experience after the last stages of death are complete.

The Death Process

Often when I arrive at a hospice patient's bedside, they are in what is known as a non-responsive state. This means they do not necessarily directly respond in a verbal or physical manner to anyone in their presence. That does not, however, mean that their full essence is non-responsive. In fact, the foundational energies that make up the spirit as well as the body are all busy at work and very aware of any presence in the room. When a person is in the death experience, they move through a step-by-step process of shutting down all supporting energies. This includes all structures we explored earlier: the dimensions of light, the chakra system, and the aura. When the time comes, all of these structures collectively transmute and return power fully back to Source. If we look at the process through *psychic energy eyes,* we can understand the forces still at work and find ways to connect with our loved one throughout the death experience.

When I work to assist a dying person, it is very similar to the work I perform on a living client. I concentrate to move energy and remove blocks found within the chakras and auric bodies to improve the flow of life-force. Even at this point in the human experience, the shifting of energies is beneficial to the health and happiness of the human body. In this instance, however, the benefit is to help the human body transition back to spirit, to facilitate the journey.

When shifting energies of someone who is dying, I find as the human body progresses toward physical death, each dimension of light, energy body, and corresponding chakra clears any old fear or dis-ease. It then slows the input of energy fully releasing the consciousness, shuts down completely, and then eventually dissipates. For the process of complete transition to occur, the influences of each individual energy body and chakra must be resolved and released. This occurs through nine different levels of transition. The first seven levels directly relate to each chakra. I have included a summary of the chakras along with the influences and imbalances our human bodies encounter during their life and death experiences as it relates to each chakra. Imbalance happens when the truth in the current energy of the meat-and-bone body does not align with the truth of the chakra consciousness. This is how a human body begins to disconnect from its Source fuel, and ultimately, if this disease continues—this will *disease* the body accordingly. Remember, disease can be physical, emotional, mental, or spiritual.

During the actual death process, the person will still have to clear any imbalance within the chakras—and find true alignment in order for that energy center to close and release.

The Ingredients of the Layer Cake

In previous chapters, we envisioned the concept of co-creation as layers and layers of consciousness, which is much like a chart of linear lines, one on top of the other. We, as the human form, experience life from the point of perception way down on the bottom of this layer cake, through a third-dimensional frame of reference (3-D) or third from the bottom. Again, there is no value system attached to these numbers. The layers represent the planes of vibrational energy or dimensions of light consciousness. For most of us, our connection to the human experience really only involves a knowing of the layers 1-3. These dimensions interact directly with the first three chakras, known as our Physical Chakras. The fourth dimension is known as the Bridge Chakra, and it is what connects our physical self to our spiritual self. The Spiritual Chakras connect to dimensions 5-7 and beyond.

The Physical Chakras: 1, 2, and 3

1st Chakra: Root/Base
Location: tailbone/perineum
Influences: self-worth, mental stability, sense of security, sense of safe, and fight-or-flight response

Imbalances (negative characteristics): digestive disorders, constipation, hemorrhoids, immunity related disorders, varicose veins, skeletal problems, osteoporosis, pain in legs and feet, lower back pain, rectal tumors, stress related ailments, allergic reactions, depression, self-esteem issues, social order, and security issues

The root chakra activates *planetary consciousness* and its relationship to Mother Earth.

Planetary consciousness is a difficult concept. It can be challenging for most of us to understand that we are actually part of the planet we call Earth. This chakra was originally designed with a consciousness that told our human body that we were *safe and connected.* That we could just *be*—we were designed as human BEings that were meant to be connected to a planetary consciousness. But eons ago, we broke this connection and replaced it with a false version of "safe." We are forever trying to find safety as a human meat-and bone-body—not realizing that the safety we crave is actually within our meat and bones. Instead, we look outward for our safety; we look to jobs, relationships, money, status, our looks, forever searching only to find frustration in UNfulfillment.

We initially upload these beliefs from those we grew up with by watching, listening, and learning *their* version of safe. We are much like a supercomputer that stores and runs these tidbits of information which we hold within our container of beliefs as we play out each day. The problem is most of the beliefs we run through our computer are someone else's and don't necessarily bring us the safety and connection we need. Unless we do the work to examine our belief systems and choose beliefs that align with our truth, we will continue to remain unfulfilled.

During the death process, if you have not examined your true beliefs and lived your own version of them, it can be difficult to release your beliefs and properly shut down the root chakra when the time comes. This can include beliefs around self-worth, purpose, material things and "stuff," status, and money.

> **2nd Chakra:** Sacral
> **Location:** halfway between pubic bone and navel
> **Influences:** reproduction, creativity, joyfulness, and enthusiasm
> **Imbalances (negative characteristics):** menstrual pain, inflammation of ovaries and cysts, sexual ailments or fungus, bladder or uterine ailments, digestive problems, ulcers, prostrate and testicular problems, impotence, diabetes, hypoglycemia, kidney problems, lower back pain, pain in hip joints, skin problems, anger, menace, hatred, apathy, blame, guilt, greed, power, control, and morality

The sacral chakra activates *emotion, joy, and relationships.*

Originally, this chakra was designed to allow our meat-and-bone bodies to feel, sense, and emote. We, however, have broken the true connection with this chakra eons ago, much like the root chakra. The human race has become think-feelers. We are much more comfortable thinking than feeling. In fact, we really don't know how to feel true deep feeling much at all. If I asked you how you feel about something, most of the time the response would be "Fine, OK, good." Most human beings don't have the capacity to connect to our true feeling center. Plus, most of us are also programmed as to how to feel depending on that initial root chakra belief system we are running: *not in this family, we don't do it that way, you have to, you need to, you should,* and so forth.

Humans were originally designed to be a feeling race—this is what makes us so unique, and yet we have allowed ourselves to become desensitized to this divine aspect of self. With regard to relationships, this chakra facilitates our ability to relate to all things around us, not necessarily just a person-to-person experience. Most of us only perceive relationships as things we do with another human, often expecting or needing another to "complete us" and that is not what this chakra was originally designed to offer. It is more about how we relate to everything, including the elements of nature itself.

During the death process, this chakra release can be difficult for those who have unfinished business or unsettled emotional relationships. Oftentimes the dying person fights exiting this plane of existence because they worry about those relationships and people they are leaving behind.

3rd Chakra: Solar Plexus
Location: 1-2" below where the ribs meet
Influences: digestion, expansiveness, growth, self-confidence and ego power, self-control, and humor
Imbalances (negative characteristics): stomach ailments or ulcers, liver, spleen or gallbladder problems, digestive problems, obesity or anorexia, heartburn, stomachaches, back pain, nervous disorders, self-esteem, fear of rejection, oversensitivity to criticism, self-image fears, nervousness, and poor memory

The solar plexus chakra activates *mental consciousness* and the physical reality of 3-D.

Again, we find the human race out of balance as a whole in this chakra. We were originally designed to have a mental consciousness that fully embraced the idea we are co-creators with Source. We, however, don't comprehend this concept, much less allow ourselves true divine power, so instead we created another power: the mental state of the ego. The ego manipulates the energies of the solar plexus through being a control freak or a victim. The controller wants to continually feel they are in charge and often wants others to see it their way—they tend to make lists for their lists and the mental monkey mind is always chattering away. The victim is at the opposite end of the spectrum, feeling as if they have no power, but in truth, they are choosing to give their power away.

During the death process, this chakra release can be extremely difficult for those who find their ego out of balance. Letting go of control is difficult for many, and when dying, this can play out in numerous scenarios. This can include fighting against letting go of material gain, status, relationships, and people, but also anger, fear, and other emotional attachments held in the controlling-mind.

The Bridge Chakra: 4

4th Chakra: Heart
Location: centered 2" above where ribs meet
Influences: circulation, love for the self and others, passion, devotion, forgiveness, and compassion
Imbalances (negative characteristics): coronary illness and heart attack, asthma and breathing disorders, lung cancer, pneumonia, colds, allergies, high or low blood pressure, elevated cholesterol, breast cancer, shoulder pain, backache in ribcage, rheumatism in arms and hands, confidence, hope, despair, hate, envy, fear, jealousy, and passivity

The bridge or heart chakra activates *feelings of unconditional love*, connecting the spiritual and physical dimensions.

The bridge chakra is all about unconditional love which is a foreign concept to most of us as we put conditions on almost every form of love there is. We humans live in a world of "*I am loved only if I…*" or "*I am not loved because I didn't…*"

We also only comprehend giving and taking love from another human, when in fact we can find love-fuel from something as simple as the beauty of a flower or the gentle breeze. Not realizing how simple unconditional love can be keeps many of us feeling unfulfilled and disconnected in the heart.

The bridge chakra connects the lower three chakras that comprise the physical consciousness energy vortexes to the top three that hold spiritual consciousness. The bridge is the astral dimension, dream place, or the plane where we house Source itself within the human form. It is the place of all potentiality.

During the death process, the release of this chakra means the actual physical death will be culminating soon. For those who feel a lot of conditions attached to receiving or giving love, learned and held as initial core belief systems, this can be a somewhat difficult transition.

The Spiritual Chakras: 5, 6 and 7

5th Chakra: Throat
Location: the notch below the Adam's Apple
Influences: communication, independence, self-expression, sense of security, loyalty, organization, and planning
Imbalances (negative characteristics): throat pain, tonsillitis, mouth ulcers, laryngitis, voice problems, gum or tooth problems, swollen glands, thyroid imbalances, fevers, flu, neck or shoulder pain, scoliosis, speech defects, addiction, criticism, faith, and problems with decision making

The throat chakra activates a transcendence of individuality where *"you"* and *"I"* now become a *"we."*

The throat is the first level of the spiritual chakras. This chakra understands duality on a higher scale—that you *are you,* I *am I,* but we *are all a collective we.* The throat chakra also houses unconditional truth and communication. Most humans are very programmed in this chakra as we are told *what to believe* and how to believe from the initial stages of our existence per others' paradigm of beliefs. We house these uploaded beliefs as we mature and begin to take them on as our own, and if we have not done a good job of re-examining these to discover if they are indeed our own, we find that the transition of this chakra can be difficult.

Many humans fight their way through life and death with regard to truths. Fighting to make others see that their version of truth is "right," not realizing another's version may indeed be their own "right." This fifth level is when our consciousness fully *remembers* that we are all right in our own version of reality—yet if the lower chakras are still carrying any ego programming, the person may struggle at this stage with "right" versus "not right."

During the death process, when this chakra releases, we let go of our individual physicality and begin to communicate with higher dimensions of existence to assist us in transitioning through this phase. We fully release any need to be "right."

6th Chakra: Third-Eye/Brow
Location: center of forehead, 1" above eyebrows
Influences: co-ordination, clarity on an intuitive level, intuition, and sense of trust
Imbalances (negative characteristics): headaches, migraines, brain tumors, strokes, poor eyesight or blindness, seizures, learning disabilities, sleep disorders, deafness or hearing impairments, colds, sinus problems, mental illness, discipline, judgment, concept of reality, confusion and pride, arrogance, suspicion, and emotional intelligence

The third-eye chakra activates the *Realm of Sacred Geometry* where all things manifest and form.

Even trying to comprehend what the *Realm of Sacred Geometry* is can be difficult, much less believing it is a part of us, within us, and that it indeed is our consciousness.

All things manifest begin with thought, vibration, and consciousness. We will see this in the crown chakra description. After thought energy, that vibration moves through a phase of the mechanics to Become. It is a layer or plane of existence where the energy comes together much like a mathematical sequence to become structure or formation. It is like the building blocks of Becoming. It is our intuitive psychic center. However, all chakras are considered psychic centers in some regard.

During the death process, this level is already so high in consciousness, that usually this clears very easily unless the programming in the initial belief systems that directly relate to the consciousness of this chakra are opposing or struggling. Most people experience this as a relatively fast transition in the dying process.

7th Chakra: Crown
Location: top of head
Influences: inner knowing and wisdom, being-ness, universal consciousness, and integration of the whole

Imbalances (negative characteristics): headaches, epilepsy, multiple sclerosis, weak immune system, mystical depression, right/left brain disorders and coordination problems, photo-sensitivity, mental illness, senility, forgetfulness, sleep disorders, lack of values, ethics, and lack of purpose

The crown chakra activates the *Harmonics of Creation* itself.

When trying to understand this concept, I like to again refer to the layer cake of consciousness to assist in this visual of how this energy moves and works. Remember in the third chakra and dimension of existence where we reside as a human form, we are very low on the cake. At the point where the crown chakra resides, we are at the top of the cake resonating as a high vibration—closest to the Source and soul. The Harmonics of Creation can be thought of as the divine mind of Source. All things manifest originally from a thought vibration, and our initial thoughts move from this dimension of existence back down through that layer cake into the sixth to become manifest in geometric shape and continue to move downward. As we move into the physical chakras of 1, 2, and 3, those thought forms have now become "real" so to speak, manifesting into form and experience. Every single moment of our existence, we are moving thought patterns into reality because of how we move this energy through our chakras.

During the death process, this level, as well as any above, is so high in consciousness-vibration, it usually clears simultaneously with ease and grace.

Summary

When shifting energies of a dying person, I find as the human body progresses toward physical death, each dimension of light, chakra, and corresponding aura and energy body clears any old fear or dis-ease. It then slows the input of energy, fully releasing the consciousness, shuts down completely, and then eventually dissipates. For the process of complete transition to occur, the influences of each individual chakra and auric energy body must be resolved and released. This occurs through nine different levels of transition. The first three chakras to transition are known as our Physical Chakras and connect us to our planetary existence. The fourth is known as the Bridge Chakra and it is what connects our physical self to our spiritual self. The last three in the body are known as the Spiritual Chakras connecting to dimensions 5-7, and the final two dimensions move beyond fully back to Spirit.

During the actual death process, the dying person will still have to clear any imbalance within the chakras—and find true alignment in order for that energy center to close and release.

PART II

Levels of Transition

Levels of Transition

At the time of our death, our soul contract has determined our mission is complete for this particular incarnation and we no longer need Source fuel to keep the body running in this 3-D experience. Just like our minds contain an instruction set for how to co-create and embody a physical form, they also contain an instruction set for how to release from the physical body and return back to Source. During our birth, each chakra activates to allow Source energy to flow. The death process is the reverse: each chakra deactivates and stops the flow. This is why I call it a process. We move through a series of stages or transitions as each chakra and auric energy body shuts down and releases consciousness.

In the pages ahead, we will look at the transitions of the death process. I've outlined these transitions only as a model of a typical death experience. Each person's process is an individual journey; some move through the stages in a methodical manner, while others create their own unique version. I've found that most people I work with in hospice followed this outline to some extent. Sometimes the person will jump from chakra to chakra, but ultimately each chakra will have to move through this process in order to fully transition back to Source energy. I have added a Case Study following each stage of transition to help you see how this information can be experienced in real life. These stories are to be used only as an example of a true transition I witnessed as a hospice volunteer.

Before we examine each transition, it's important to understand that each chakra and auric energy body plays a specific role in helping us release our physical bodies as well as our individual minds. Odd numbered chakras (1, 3, 5, and 7) relate to our physical connections. They hold our physical relationship to the

AN ENERGY HEALER'S BOOK OF DYING

Earth, humanity, the universe, and Source. When these chakras and auric energy bodies shut down, they allow us to release our physical ties. Chakras 2, 4, 6, and 8 are connected to the mind. They hold everything we've created through our thoughts and mental processes. When these chakras shut down, they allow us to release all we've co-created in this life. Think of it this way: odd numbered chakras release *"all we experience* as the physical *BODY."* Even numbered chakras release *"all we create* as the *MIND."*

This is how the levels of transition break out for release during the death process:

Body Releases include Chakras 1, 3, 5, and 7

Chakra 1 ~ First Level of Transition:
Shuts down the consciousness of *"all we experience* as the physical *BODY"* related to Earth and the planet.

Chakra 3 ~ Third Level of Transition:
Shuts down the consciousness of *"all we experience* as the physical *BODY"* related to humanity.

Chakra 5 ~ Fifth Level of Transition:
Shuts down the consciousness of *"all we experience* as the physical *BODY"* related to the greater universe.

Chakra 7 ~ Seventh Level of Transition:
Shut down of *"all we experience* as the physical *BODY"* related to celestial soul.

Mind Releases include Chakras 2, 4, 6, and 8

Chakra 2 ~ Second Level of Transition:
Final Release of *"all we create* as the *MIND"* related to Earth and the planet.

Chakra 4 ~ Fourth Level of Transition:
Final Release of *"all we create* as the *MIND"* related to humanity.

Chakra 6 ~ Sixth Level of Transition:
Final Release of *"all we create* as the *MIND"* related to the greater universe.

Chakra 8 ~ Eighth Level of Transition:
Final release of *"all we create* as the *MIND"* related to celestial soul.

To me, the concept of shutting off the fuel and releasing our connection to planet Earth, humanity, universe, and celestial soul demonstrates how much we are one with our Source. As a living, breathing experience of Source energy, we actively co-create the planet, humanity, universe, and celestial soul each and every day. We choose to connect to them to live as one, and we then choose to dis-connect from them when it is time to return back home. When you really sit with this concept, our brief human existence becomes quite magical indeed.

My goal in breaking out the elements of each transition is to help those in the presence of a loved one's journey find a sense of awe and wonder in the process, as opposed to sitting in anger or fear. My hope is that people will talk about death freely and without undue sadness while witnessing or experiencing it. Through the lens of *psychic sight*, we can resist the urge to feel fear when a loved one is dying because we'll know there is nothing *but* life.

We can honor the process by understanding that life in one's present physical form is a wondrous gift that our loved one chose to experience as a *body and a divine mind* for this concrete period of time only—and now they are choosing once again to experience another version of Source.

If you are fortunate enough to be in the presence of one's death journey, try to see if you can not only sense the energy of the journey, but also the energy of the magic of the room, the light, the spirits, the Source.

Summary

During our birth, each chakra and auric energy body activates to allow Source energy to flow. The death process is the reverse: each center deactivates and stops the flow. We move through a series of stages or transitions as each chakra shuts down and releases consciousness. Each chakra plays a specific role in helping us release our physical bodies as well as our individual minds. Odd numbered chakras (1, 3, 5, and 7) relate to our physical connections. They hold our physical relationship to the Earth, humanity, the universe, and Source. When these chakras shut down, they allow us to release our physical ties. Chakras 2, 4, 6, and 8 are connected to the mind. They hold everything we've created through our thoughts and mental processes. When these chakras shut down, they allow us to release all we've co-created in this life. Think of it this way: odd-numbered chakras release "*all we experience* as the physical *BODY*." Even-numbered chakras release "*all we create* as the *MIND*."

Note on Stages of Transition

This book describes the process of death in "order" for teaching purposes; however, the steps in transition may or may not move in the order as described. Many times, the dying person will move through the stages in a methodical way; yet for others, the dying process may jump from one chakra to another, skipping some and returning to others. There is no right or wrong way.

First Level of Transition

1st Dimension of Light / Root Chakra / Auric Etheric Body
Shuts down the consciousness of *"all we experience"* as the *BODY* of Mother Earth Energies and Planet Consciousness

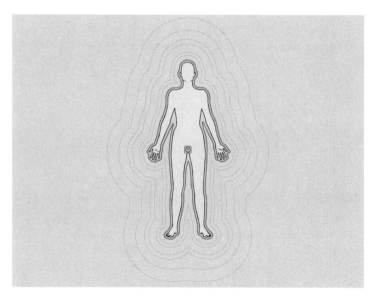

Root Chakra and Auric Etheric Body

The root chakra is the last to ignite during gestation and typically the first to de-ignite in death. The first chakra holds our connection to the Earth throughout our life. When we enter the dying process, we first release this physical connection to Mother Earth by:

- Shutting down consciousness of living out the experience of Mother Earth and planetary consciousness.

- Shutting down consciousness of planet and the relationship to it including all life forms.
- Shutting down the first dimension of light: the collective. consciousness and planetary consciousness, emotional in nature.
- Shutting down and then dissolving the root chakra or base chakra.
- Shutting down and then dissolving the auric etheric energy body.

For those assisting anyone through the death process, you may witness varying levels of the dying person's fear or struggle with some of the following:

- Fear of leaving their home, things, or *stuff*.
- Fear of not enough money or lost sense of security.
- Fear of loss of control.
- Releasing of family beliefs, societal beliefs, and religious dogma beliefs.

When we begin the first level of transition, we are working in an experience *AS A BODY* where the first auric field and root chakra hold our life-force energy that is aligned with the first dimension of light, the planetary collective consciousness. This consciousness is all about why we are here on the planet. It examines why and how we assist Mother Earth with our energy fields and our body. The dying person is at a point in their Earth-walk where they have basically finished their planetary contract and responsibilities. Therefore, the initial stages of releasing the physical body from the Earth plane commences.

In working with the first levels of energy, we will find the person potentially encountering any unresolved physical function, self-worth, and security-based issues. These are most likely matters of letting go of *things or stuff*. This can be a very fearful period for many as the loss of material items creates a sense of panic. Panic and fear come from the ego and ingrained beliefs that tell me I am somebody because of what I do, what I have, or what my body is like or not like. It is a very physical chakra which involves the release of family beliefs, societal beliefs, religious dogma beliefs, and other beliefs we have taken on during this incarnation. The release of this chakra is only the initial stage of the process. It can take quite some time, especially if the person has many unresolved issues and beliefs. It can oftentimes be fear-based, especially with regard to money and worth issues. This is a time when the person is still somewhat coherent, able to understand and semi-converse. Coherent or not, the energy work I perform is the same both verbally and mentally. It is a time to ease their fears and assure them that everything will be okay.

It is a time to be present for the dying person. I work to share unconditional love in order to assist shifting the energy of the person and the physical space. Any family member, friend, or medical attendant can do the same by being there physically, emotionally, mentally, and spiritually for the person. This is done with a nonjudgmental gift of sharing divine love. Verbal and physical communication, telepathic conversation, or prayer will all work to assist in this situation. The person often needs (and wants) permission to move beyond this fear which is based in ego. Each person moves through this transition level at their own pace. Some take days, and some take hours.

Communication Reminder

Communicating true feeling is a difficult thing for many, especially when it comes to emotionally sensitive subjects that arise when faced with the process of death. Remember, if you are not comfortable with verbally articulating your thoughts and emotions with the one dying or those in attendance, expressing your thoughts and feelings telepathically is an option.

We all have the gift of telepathic communication, meaning the ability to transmit and receive information from one mind to another without using auditory words or physical interaction.

For me, this is another form of prayer. Simply silently speak and hold your truth inside of your mind and heart without the need to express it out loud. In this way, your Higher Self is directly communicating with your loved one's Higher Self and there is no need to side-step or soften your true feelings, allowing you a safe way to fully express your true feelings and say what you need to say. The vibrational frequency of your message will align with the loved one's higher knowing, and oftentimes that knowledge or message is heard by the dying person's conscious or subconscious self.

Regardless of whether or not you perceive your message being received on the physical plane, it is still communicated in the higher realms and offers you, the sender, the energetic release of closure.

What I telepathically see is an eventual release of old energy patterns and a clearing of the field and chakra. At this phase, there is not much in the way of color within the auric fields throughout the room. I often feel a dense energy throughout their surroundings at this point. As mentioned above, this transition of the root chakra slowing to the point of stopping can often take a number of hours and sometimes days to shift and move. Eventually, it will stop and then go dark. The auric etheric body, which looks somewhat like a fine blueprint, will begin to dissipate. With this release, the first dimension of light dissolves. At this time, the dying person is releasing the blueprint, or instruction set, of their human body overall. They are releasing their planetary consciousness, their life-force-energies, and their entire relationship to Mother Earth itself. They are releasing all security-related human experiences. The details of *"all they experienced"* in this current lifetime will begin to transform into an energetic file of sorts.

This file is information for their final Akashic Record which now includes their body experience and relationship with Mother Earth. This first level of transition occurs to shut down all Earth energies as the body of the co-created experience. As we move to the next level, we will see how these same Earth energies will transition as a final release in their journey to the second level.

What I *Psychically* See at this Level

During this time, I psychically *see* an energetic release within the human body in terms of the person's programmed belief systems. This happens in the lower trunk of the body—the hips, the legs, the "meat and bone" of the body. The colors of the energy throughout the room that the person is in usually feels to me somewhat dense and oftentimes fear-based. This can be a heavy feeling. A thick feeling. The more fear the person carries in their field, the thicker the energy of the room. The actual auric colors of the energy within the room are somewhat like muddy or charcoal blobs that move in slow patterns.

As I work to assist the dying person through this phase, their root or base chakra will eventually slow to the point of stopping and then it will go dark. My job is to support them in releasing any fears with regards to *stuff* and material things—knowing that their possessions are no longer important. I also work to help them know they are safe. That all is OK with allowing their body to progress through this journey. Telepathically talking them through this concept helps to release any energy blocks.

As they continue to release any blocks holding these programmed patterns of beliefs, eventually their first dimension of light will dissolve as does their etheric body of the aura. It is a transmuting of energy—a returning to Source.

What Your Loved One *May Be* Psychically Experiencing at this Level

Because this chakra release usually happens at the beginning levels of transition, the dying person is typically experiencing more 3-D encounters with their own programmed beliefs rather than interaction with spirit-helpers (who will arrive to assist in later stages).

Confronting personal beliefs can give rise to mental and emotional fears that play out much like a reel of memories, similar to an old-time movie speeding through the person's consciousness container. If the person encountered fear-based people, places, and situations throughout their life, this movie reel offers the ability to examine, forgive, and release these experiences.

Most of the psychic connections the dying person brings forth at this level have to do with revisiting their sense of safety, BEing, and self-worth.

Healing Strategies for this Level

- Allow yourself to be as present as much as you choose for your loved one, either in person or from afar, *only when balanced with making sure you take care of yourself* in terms of nourishment, sleep, and support.
- If there is any unfinished business with the person, try your best to resolve these issues, if possible. If that is not possible, try to write down your unresolved business, and release any negative holds via prayer, a burning ceremony, or whatever you choose to do to allow the issues to move onward.
- As the caregiver, allow yourself to go through all the emotions, feelings, and stages of grieving.
- Do your best through conversation to reassure your loved one that all of their things will be taken care of—their home, their belongings, their treasures—offering them solace that they can let go of *stuff.*
- Express your thoughts and feelings with your loved one, either out loud or in your heart.

First Level Case Study:
How and Why We Hold On

The death process is an amazing thing to me. It always has been and always will be, I am sure. One of the special ways I get to share my psychic gifts in working with the dying is by assisting them so that they might experience an easier passing physically, emotionally, mentally, and spiritually. My hospice experiences are many, but one of my most memorable is that of a woman in her very late 80s or early 90s. The hospice caregivers were in a bit of a quandary as to what to do with this patient, as she had been actively dying for quite some time, and yet was having difficulty in ending her journey. At the point when they asked for my assistance, her body had been fully non-responsive for quite some time, and was no longer accepting any medicine or food and barely even water for over 30 days. Medically, they were at a loss as to why she was still holding on and wanted me to see if I could get answers telepathically as to what was keeping her here on the physical plane.

Death can be a difficult journey in so many ways, not only for the person dying, but sometimes for their caregivers as well. This particular case was an "in-home" patient, although normally I work in a nursing home or hospital environment. The daughter, the primary care-giver and resident, greeted me at the door. As we made our way through the home, the thick intense energy of the death process filled the air. The vibration throughout the home was heavy and dense, which indicated to me that the patient was struggling even though her physical body showed no signs of a fight. In fact, her physical body showed not much of anything at all since she had actively been dying for over a month. She was so tiny and frail, completely unresponsive, and looked to be asleep. Her size and frame were almost child-like. She had a peacefulness to her face and her breathing was so slight and shallow, it was difficult to even recognize it. She was an African American woman pushing ninety years, and yet she had the most beautiful flawless skin, barely a wrinkle, with a glow emanating love and light.

Her family had done a tremendous job of holding vigil for her, but they were now showing signs of the ongoing strain and stress of the death watch of thirty-plus days. They were tired, frustrated, and had no answers as to why their dear mother would not surrender to her passing. All the family members had given her permission to go, many times over in fact, and yet she silently held on. Her struggle was not physically apparent, but obviously her spirit was strong-willed enough to hold her body hostage for much too long.

I entered her bedroom—her vigil abode, and sat quietly with the daughter and tapped into the energies of the room and the patient. When I do hospice work, I telepathically work in silence to assist the patient in shifting their energies. I search to find whatever energy block may be prohibiting their passing and then I release that energy to assist them in moving forward through the process of dying. I normally keep this work to myself and private from the family, but the moment I sat down, the daughter looked me straight in the eye and said, "*You know things…*"

I shared some information of my psychic gifts with her, explaining that I was an energy practitioner who basically shifts energy fields to assist in any way needed. Once the conversation opened up, the daughter continued to ask me many questions about what information I got on her mother. I have no access to any medical files on this case or any patient, and yet I told this daughter many things that were true about her mother. I knew that she was extremely attached to her home, the actual physical structure. When scanning her energy fields and by communicating with her telepathically, I found that the reason she did not let go was because she did not understand how to let go of her physical world and mostly her home. She did not know how to leave this space. This is where she felt safe.

This energy block is found in the programmed consciousness held in the initial root chakra—the first chakra that houses our belief systems. This patient fully believed that the physical structure of her brick and mortar home for 30+ years was her "safe" and did not comprehend a world without it. The daughter further shared with me that her mother had not been able to physically leave that very home for the past thirty years, that she had become agoraphobic and had not left for anyone or anything. The confusion of how to release this mental belief system was the actual energetic vibration that was struggling and permeating the physical home—the energy pattern I had felt immediately upon my arrival. Not knowing how to let go of a brick and mortar structure was part of the reason this beautiful tiny woman could not allow her consciousness to fully return to Source energy and I needed to find a way to assist her.

I worked with this patient over the next hour or so to release belief patterns regarding her sense of survival, security, possessions, and structure. I left that evening telling the daughter I would return in one or two days if she had not passed to again revisit the scenario. She was still alive two days later, when I returned to find the last reason she had not yet *fully* let go.

During that second visit, I returned to her bedroom and again tapped in to the energies of the patient. I immediately sensed that she had indeed let go of the concept of the brick and mortar structure, but there was an additional energy block now residing in her sacral chakra that also was holding this beautiful woman hostage to the death process. I asked the daughter if her deceased father had spent time in the room across the hall from the mother's room because I could still feel his energy signature within the home. She indicated that it was the room where her father had died a couple of years back. I shared with her that some fragments of her father's energy were still in the home. He was by no means a "ghost energy" haunting in any way—but a bit too much of his essence still held on to the relationship of the home and the dying mother. This ultimately was affecting the patient's passing as she did not know how to leave her husband's energy that still resided within the home.

First, I worked with the consciousness of the father to fully cross him over, explaining to him that his wife would indeed be with him when they both crossed.

Second, I further worked with the woman to fully explain the scenario and assure her that all would be fine when they both went fully to the light. When I left that evening, I knew she would be gone by the next morning, and indeed she was. And I am certain they were fully reunited on the other side, together once again.

First Level Summary

- It is a fearful period for many and can be confusing.
- Loss of material items may create a sense of panic.
- This is a time to be fully present for the dying person.
- Share unconditional love to assist family, friend, or medical attendant by working physically, emotionally, mentally, and spiritually.

- Assist your loved one with verbal or telepathic conversation or prayer.
- This is the beginning stage of the death process in energy and usually takes a number of hours, days or weeks to transition.

Second Level of Transition

2nd Dimension of Light / Sacral Chakra / Auric Emotional Body
Final Release of *"all we create"* as the *MIND* of Mother Earth Energies and Planet Consciousness

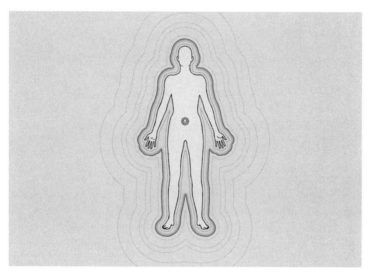

Sacral Chakra and Auric Emotional Body

Throughout our lives, we continuously work to co-create and influence our planet. During the second transition, we release all we have created while being a part of Earth, including all Earth-bound relationships and our relationship with the Earth itself. This stage includes the:

• Final release of consciousness to send home the final Akashic Record of Mother Earth.

- Final release of assistance to manifest the world.
- Final release of energies of earth, wind, water, and fire.
- Final release of the second dimension of light: the collective unconscious, mental in nature.
- Shutting down and then dissolving the sacral chakra.
- Shutting down and then dissolving the auric emotional energy body.

For those assisting anyone through the death process, you may witness varying levels of the dying person's fear or struggle with some of the following:

- The person can become agitated during this time depending on the personal relationships they have experienced.
- They may also be concerned about those loved ones who are or are not present, so assuring them all is OK is important.
- This is also a time when they begin to really attach to beliefs they grew up with in terms of the afterlife.

This second phase continues the process of letting go. We are working to release an experience *as the mind* of Mother Earth energies and planet consciousness. The second chakra is our feelings and emotions center. It releases all sensing and feeling energies. Its auric field is the emotional body. This level resides in the second dimension of light, a collective unconscious energy that mediates between the heart of Earth and heart of humanity. This transition releases our individual energies we have used to harness the elements of earth, water, air, and fire to assist in our relationship with Mother Nature in manifesting our planet. The individual is starting the process of bodily leaving the physical earth, and because of this, they are emotionally and energetically releasing the relationship to Mother Earth. Most of us go through our entire lifespan without even realizing our connection to the planet, but our subconscious and Higher Self is fully aware of this and is now allowing it to release. It is also a time when we are emotionally releasing Earth-bound relationships. When people let go of emotional blocks, this can involve unresolved issues they may be holding onto with family, friends, and loved ones they will be leaving behind when they pass. Relationships—good, bad, and ugly—which we are leaving often are hard to let go of. Sometimes I come across a person who is harboring fear of encountering a deceased relative or friend from the other side who they are hesitant to meet again. Sometimes it is fear of the beliefs and the relationships we have been taught with regard to God, heaven, or hell.

To assist the person through this phase, we can only offer similar tactics we used in clearing the first chakra: unconditional sharing of divine love. Most often they are holding onto family members and friends, so again, verbal and physical communication, telepathic conversation, or prayer to allow the person permission to let go of relationships is key. Family and friends can help by sending the message in love to the person that those left behind will be okay when they leave. And remember again, give them permission to move forward.

The timeline of this stage is very personal to each situation. This period usually includes a major unplugging of ego-belief issues on the dying person's part. It is the time when the dying person lets go of friends and family who have potentially powered their ego in the past (good or bad). If the person is working in a fear state, they worry they cannot leave family members and friends for one reason or another. This can be a very ego-related release time. If that is the case, there will be a real pull-effect to the energies within the room. I often look for any energetic cords attached to their living family and friends that the person may be holding on to and work to release them. This is a time to set free ego-based and human-based relationships. These relationships will still be there in energy when the loved one dies, just utilizing another higher level of consciousness.

Those who are involved with a loved one's dying process can really assist in this stage of energy movement by emotionally letting go of the human existence of the person, emotionally allowing them to die. By doing this, they can let go of any energetic cords they may hold on that person. Examining the ego of those left living is critical.

We don't want to lose our loved one (because we make it about us) and yet they get to die, and if we can allow ourselves to honor that concept, this phase is easier on everyone.

There can be a very distinct shift in energy for not only the person dying, but the supporting energy within the room when we allow this gift of letting go to occur. The density of the energies in the room will dissipate or shift. Sometimes I find myself with a person who energetically leaves their physical body at this time to energetically *go and see* a loved one elsewhere before they choose to move onward. I have worked with dying people in transition who have energetically-psychically gone to visit loved ones far away, while indeed their physical body is sitting right there in the room with me. I like to refer to this as a fly-by situation. I believe this is why sometimes we get an odd, unexplained sense that a loved one is passing when we may not know or even be anywhere near them at the time. We just feel it and usually find out at a later time we were right.

I believe this particular energetic transition is something we all should understand. Sometimes, we may not be able to physically be at the bedside of those we love when they are dying. This can bring guilt and sadness to many of the loved ones not able to get there "in time" or not being able to be holding vigil in person. The dying person energetically knows you are there for them.

Their consciousness is expanding to an omnipresent state, and you physically being at bedside is not important in this transition. Energetically, the fly-by scenario allows us the opportunity to remember we are all connected in energy at all times. The human ego of the friends and family that are left behind is a struggle with their own personal grieving energy and angst of the situation. For most people, from a Higher Self perspective, bedside attendance is not an issue. In fact, many dying people fully choose to die alone.

As the second chakra clears, I can often see the energies letting go from the belly area of the dying person. When clear, the sacral chakra will slow to the point of stopping, and it will then go dark. What I see at this time in the human aura is darkness to the lower portion of the human form. The energy body that is releasing is the auric emotional body. As this body dissolves, so does the second dimension of light. There are not any auric movements above the body and not much happening in energies throughout the room.

At this time, the person is sealing the file of information in their Akashic Record of *"all they created"* for their emotional planetary experience of humanness and humanity as well as their relationship to the Earth elements. This energetic file of information will return to spirit and become content for the individual's Book of Life. This second level of transition occurs as a final release of all Earth energies as the mind of creation. As we move to the next level, we will see how we move toward the shut-down of human form energies in their journey to the third level.

What I *Psychically* See at this Level

During this time, I psychically *see* an energetic release within the human body in the belly area. The actual auric colors of the energy within the room are still somewhat like muddy blobs that move in slow patterns, but as we move through this phase, the patterns will begin to take on a bit of a lighter flow. Also, the fields of energy will begin to bring in a bit of color into the blobs of energy moving throughout the room.

As I work to assist the dying person through this phase, their sacral chakra will eventually slow to the point of stopping and then it will go dark. My job is to assist them in releasing any concerns with relationships, emotions, and fears. This can be a difficult time for many to let go of their loved ones, so I also work to help them know they are safe, as are any loved ones that they may be leaving behind. Telepathically talking them through this concept helps to release any energy blocks.

As they continue to release, their second dimension of light will dissolve as does their emotional body of the aura. It is a transmuting of energy—a returning to Source.

What Your Loved One *May Be* Psychically Experiencing at this Level

During this stage, your loved one continues to release 3-D beliefs and programming, but now the focus is on his or her relationships with others. I find many dying people psychically visit those who may not be in attendance with them or holding vigil for their death. The psychic self energetically is omnipresent, meaning the consciousness can astrally travel anywhere within any time-space continuum to make amends or find forgiveness for self or others.

These experiences can range from the person psychically visiting a loved one who has already passed to connecting with someone who is still in physical human form on Earth. Reasons for a psychic visit may be to atone for the past, make a love-connection, or send a message.

For some, this can be a time when they begin to better understand the process of how soul transition works in omnipresent love, meaning that whether deceased or still in the process of dying, our energy has the ability to connect with loved ones at any time and in any place. For others, the realization of omnipresent love comes much later in their transition during the heart chakra release in the fourth and fifth levels.

Healing Strategies for this Level

- Make sure you and all caregivers are getting sufficient rest, food, and fresh air.
- Talk to other family members about their feelings on the journey of your loved one and share your true feelings with them.
- Review your relationship with your loved one and see if there is anything unfinished that needs attention.
- Forgive anything that is holding any unease in any way.
- Thank your loved one for their relationship with you.
- Reassure the person that all others involved will be looked after and taken care of, allowing them to move onward with no worries.

- Express your thoughts and feelings with your loved one, either out loud or in your heart.

Second Level Case Study:
Fear for the Family

As I mentioned in the last chapter, most of my hospice patients are in a nursing home, with only a few being an in-home patient. However, this particular case was also with an in-home patient. The hospice administration called me in on this due to the fact that the family was having an extremely difficult time with the death process playing out for such an extended time in their home. This man was completely non-responsive and not able to communicate, so there was no way to understand why he was not moving forward. The caregiver-family included his young daughter, her husband, and their three young children.

The hospice nurse drove me to this home for the session, because she informed me that the home was in a very unsafe part of town and she did not want me to go alone. This area was run-down and dangerous, with the homes and families vulnerable to the surroundings.

The moment I entered the home, the energies of this death was fighting throughout the entire household. The surrounding energies of the neighborhood were also part of this fight. There was so much fear and negativity swirling about. This was also very apparent in the bedroom where the man was experiencing his final hours of physical life.

I entered the room with the daughter to find her father non-responsive with agitated breathing and struggling body motions. He had not spoken to anyone for several days, so they had no idea where he was with his journey. I began to tap into him telepathically to see what I could learn from him as to why he was in a holding pattern for his passage. It became clear very quickly that this particular gentleman had not lived an easy life. He was holding a lot of anger, fear, and tons of regret. He had not been a "very nice" person, he telepathically explained, and he now was having a difficult time being presented with the death experience and what was to come. The life with his family (including the daughter in residence) was one of pain and regret, and yet at this point he had no way to communicate any parting messages. This was part of the worry keeping him here. He was also holding an enormous amount of fear for the future of this family, especially living in the neighborhood where this home was—where his daughter and grandchildren were living. He knew it was dangerous. Safety from the neighbors directly next door was, especially, a great concern of his.

I sat with him and explained what I do and how I felt I could assist. I told him that I could also communicate his needs to his family, therefore asking for forgiveness and also sharing his concerns about their safety. I also shared with him how as an energy worker/ healer, I could rebalance the energetic grid patterns surrounding his property and provide assistance and protection from the angelic realm. I called in the shielding assistance of Archangel Michael, and together we provided a barrier of love and light, especially from the surrounding neighbors. I believe because he was in transition, he could feel the sense of protection forming around this home and felt his family would now be safe. I also gathered the family and channeled his concerns and his apologies for past events and asked for forgiveness on his behalf.

It was an intimate healing opportunity for the daughter and her husband—to make peace with this man who had lived such a difficult life, and had made such an impression on theirs.

A combination of fear, regret, and trepidation of a possible Hell to come were all very valid energetic reasons this man's journey was being restricted. The sacral chakra holds relationships, emotions, and feelings. He needed an outlet to share his feelings, ask for forgiveness, and trust that his family would be safe before he felt he could make peace with his death.

By the time I was leaving, his body movements had calmed and he was resting peacefully. The next day, I was informed by Hospice staff that he had died a couple hours after we had left, peacefully surrounded by his family.

Unfinished business, especially when it comes to relationships, unsaid truths, and unforgiven words are all things that one may want to examine when they are alive and well. The imbalanced energies that we carry in our fields that affect our lives also affect us during our death process. Something to think about.

Second Level Summary

- There is an emotional release of Earth-bound relationships.
- Emotional blocks for the person can include unresolved issues with family, friends, and loved ones.
- They may be harboring fear of encountering a deceased relative or friend.
- They may have fear of God, heaven, or hell.
- There is an ego-related release, causing a pull-effect to the energies within the room.
- It is key to assist the dying person with unconditional sharing of divine love.

Third Level of Transition

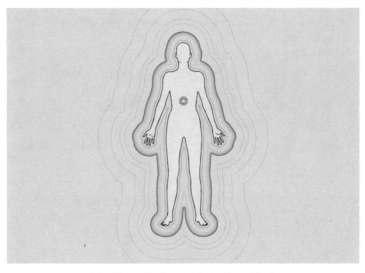

Solar Plexus Chakra and Auric Mental Body

The third chakra, the solar plexus, connects us to our physical
human form and humanity as a whole. This is where we encounter
elements of the ego.

When we release this chakra, we let go of our physical experience
as a human being by:

- Shutting down consciousness of living out the experience of
  human form.

- Shutting down the level of human consciousness that is collective with the physical realities of 3-D and connection to all physical laws.
- Shutting down individual identity of collective and realignment with Higher Self and Source.
- Shutting down the third dimension of light: the collective consciousness and human consciousness, emotional in nature.
- Shutting down and then dissolving the solar plexus chakra
- Shutting down and then dissolving the auric mental energy body.

For those assisting anyone through the death process, you may witness varying levels of the dying person's fear or struggle with some of the following:

- This can be a time when the dying person's body shows some physical changes, like jerky breathing, physically struggling, etc. Remember, this is their process of moving through the release of the auric templates.
- This is also a time when their body can show color changes on hands and feet which is the breakdown of the auric templates.
- This can be a stubborn time for some, depending on the ego of the person and their family.

The third chakra is our will center, our intuitive energy. Its field is the auric mental body working to release an experience *as a body* of the human form energies. We are letting go of the third dimension of light as a human as well as a collective consciousness of humanity as a whole. This is where we begin to release all physical realities of time and physical laws. We are starting to stage the realignment to return to our Higher Self, or celestial soul, to begin the journey "back home." The third level is a very critical shift in energy as this stage concludes the shutting down of the complete physical plane and the solar plexus chakra—the will center. We now find the person encountering their dual power sources—the *ME* of our human ego versus the *WE* of the collective Source consciousness. As we fully release from the physical plane and our human will, any remaining *ME-powered* issues of ego blocks are resolved. This indeed may be a tough transition for those with a strong ego, will, and control issues, whether they manifested as material gain and status or in relationships. The struggle to let go of what we have created or identified with is now beginning to liberate us from not only the physical, but also the emotional and mental bodies. This is also where we find some very distinctive changes happening with the body. This is the time that the person's breathing patterns become jerky, gurgling, and usually unsettling to those nearby. This is also the time when the person physically appears to be struggling. This can cause great concern to those holding vigil. The actual struggle, however, is within the realignment of power sources and ego release. The energies are working to let go of human consciousness, of any remaining *ME-related* ego power still fighting to release the concept of control so it can move to the stage of full *WE-consciousness*, where we need no ego or control.

It is again a time to be present for the dying person by sharing divine love. Any family member, friend, or medical attendant can be there physically, emotionally, mentally, and spiritually for that person to move through any ego energies holding them back. This is done with verbal and physical communication, telepathic conversation, or prayer allowing your loved one permission to move beyond this fear that is based in ego. This is a time to be patient rather than allowing our fear to judge how the physical template is letting go, even though it may seem to us that the dying person is struggling. And knowing fully that it is actually one of the most needed and wanted releases of the death process. On a higher plane, the dying person is joy-filled to be offered the opportunity to move beyond this template, even though his or her body may not necessarily represent that in the physical world. They will move through this process at their own pace, so this phase often takes patience and steadfastness from those in vigil.

We also will start to see the beginnings of mottling during this release, where the person's feet, hands, and sometimes arms begin to turn blackish-blue and blotchy. This can be scary to those holding vigil, seeing their loved one's physical form change. This mottling is happening because we all have robust energy centers or chakras in both our hands and feet directly grounding us to the Earth plane. As we shut these chakra centers down and release the consciousness from the physical plane, those main foot and hand chakras go dark, as does our body at that energy point. The dark is the template releasing. Sometimes the person's body also seems to display a web-effect of discoloration or white-ish splotches. This is the very light yellowish lines of the auric mental energy body grid dissolving throughout and around the human form. What I *see* at this time is the beginning of a very beautiful transition of energy and the release of the third dimension of light.

In this stage, the person is releasing their mental consciousness of being human, including elements of the ego. They are letting go of all 3-D realities and human laws. The energy of *"all they experienced"* as this consciousness will transform into an energetic file of information for their final Akashic Record for the experience of being a human form. This energetic file of information will return to spirit and become content for the person's Book of Life. Even though this may be a difficult time for those witnessing the process, energetically it is an important transitional stage toward a gentle, calm surrender to the spiritual plane.

Energetically speaking, it is actually one of the most beautiful, peaceful transitions of the entire process as the *full WE-collective consciousness* begins to take charge. At this point, the energy in the room may indeed feel somewhat heavy as the power sources change hands. This third level of transition *shuts down* the human form energies as the body of the experience. The next level will then be the *final release* of these human form energies. As we move toward the next stage, the person crosses the *bridge* from a physical experience toward a spiritual one in energy in their journey to the fourth level.

What I *Psychically See* at this Level

During this time, I psychically *see* an energetic release within the human body in terms of the person's programmed ego.

In my opinion, this is one of the most difficult phases for those in attendance, when ironically it is one of the most beautiful phases for the dying person. Because it is such a human release of all physical templates, the physical body seems to be struggling, however the spirit is peacefully surrendering.

Psychically, this is a stage of a beautiful transition in energy. It is a calm and gentle return to the spiritual planes of existence, yet the body can seem to be doing everything but surrendering into the calm. If you are in attendance at this time and are experiencing what you see as struggle, please note that this is similar to a snake shedding an old outgrown skin, wriggling into the freedom of a different body of existence.

The actual auric colors of the energy within the room can seem to fight during this stage as well because this is such a release of ego and physicality. Depending on the person, this energetic imbalance can be slight or significant.

As I work to assist the person through this phase, their solar plexus chakra will eventually slow to the point of stopping and then it will go dark. My job is to assist them in releasing any ego and physical fears. Telepathically talking them through this concept helps to release any energy blocks.

As they continue to release, their third dimension of light will dissolve as does their mental body of the aura. It is a transmuting of energy—a returning to Source.

What Your Loved One *May Be* Psychically Experiencing at this Level

The third level of transition can appear to be one of the most difficult times in the death process for the loved one's physical body, as many seem to struggle physically with jerking movements and rapid breath. That said, their psychical self is experiencing another side to this process.

The physical body of consciousness is beginning to fully release, which allows the dying person to remember his or her spiritual body. To the outside world this looks like a struggle, but psychically, it is an introduction of an old beloved friend: their true self. During this time in the process, the body is being flooded with love and light, and you can see this as the web-effects in the auric fields I described earlier.

For most, this is also a welcome relief of *remembering*, remembering what we know in terms of *there is more*. However, for anyone who is fear-filled in ego, power, dominance, and control, this can be a difficult remembering which may extend this chakra release time. Those holding vigil may offer understanding and support via loving thoughts and patience.

Healing Strategies for this Level

- Make sure you and all caregivers are getting sufficient rest, food, and fresh air.
- This is a time for patience for the process. It is important to remember that some of the physical changes are due to the auric template shifts, and if one can honor that transitional experience and remain calm instead of fear it, that helps the dying person.
- Ask questions of the professionals if this gives you a better sense of knowledge and comfort in this process.
- Acknowledge any of your own fears and anger away from the person's bedside; share your emotions and feelings with others available to you.
- Help others in the room share their feelings and emotions and be tolerant of their grieving processes.
- Begin a journal of your visits and leave a shared book in the room.
- Express your thoughts and feelings with your loved one, either out loud or in your heart.

Third Level Case Study:
Live as if You Are Dying

I was interviewed once on a national radio show as a hospice expert, and as the show was coming to its end, the host asked me if I had any parting words of wisdom for the audience. I replied: *"Live as if you are dying, because indeed we are. I suggest clearing and balancing your chakras while still alive because not only will you live a more divine and truth-filled life, but you most likely will experience an incredibly beautiful death, with an easy transition back to Source."* I meant every word and try my best to live my life this way and share these ideas with my clients. The following is a story about an incredible man who took that information to heart.

Sometimes in life we are gifted with the chance meeting of a person that will forever change us—*completely*. This is what happened when I met Rick, a new neighbor at my cabin. I was initially introduced to Rick through another cabin neighbor. He was about my age, married with two great girls around the same age as my kids. In his earlier years, Rick had been both an AWA and WWF wrestler, the kind of entertainer who tossed crazy costumed giants around a ring on TV every Saturday afternoon. At this time in his life, he was looking forward to building his dream home up north, with hopes of eventually retiring there within the near future.

He was a strong, stocky man with twinkling eyes and a great belly laugh. He and his family became great lake-friends and I thoroughly enjoyed his company. One of my favorite memories of Rick was when he was helping us with a trash-run to the local dump. We have an area at the lake where we collect discarded items until it is embarrassingly time to fill a trailer and make the run into the town's dump. Usually all the neighbors pitch in and help one another with this job, making it a group effort, as was the case the morning I found Rick in my junk pile hard at work before I even had my first cup of coffee. I dashed out to assist just as I witnessed Rick singularly heaving an entire steel beam up over his head like a barbell and tossing it into the trailer as if it were a simple javelin throw. What amazed me more about Rick's feat of strength was watching my three grown boys struggle to collectively lift a remaining steel beam out of the pile.

Rick's physical body had taken quite a beating all the years he entertained in the wrestling ring. His knees were a disaster, as was his back and neck. Sometimes I would make my way to his cabin to do a healing session with him to help relieve some of his chronic pain. He was very open to the idea of metaphysical work, even though he didn't really comprehend the concept of it—he just knew it helped his aching joints and allowed him more mobility.

One hot June weekend, a favorite time at the cabin for us all, Rick found himself in the emergency room in town with some pretty severe issues that ended up needing further investigation by his primary doctor in the city. Weeks later, following his tests, he and his family returned back up north and I saw him on the dock with our neighbors. As I approached the moored pontoon where they were all chatting, I heard him saying that *they were not yet sure of what was going on with him*—and that *he might entertain getting another doctor's opinion*, but he had not made his mind up to do so as yet.

Sometimes the gift of psychic sight is a double-edged sword in that you *know things* that others may not, and there are times that information is not easy for me nor any healer. There is a moral and ethical responsibility that comes with this gift. I have an ability to scan a person and feel what it is their body feels. It is called being a medical intuitive or medical empath. I can also see the aura of the person and psychically see inside of their body, sometimes revealing energy blocks or medical conditions. I really have no right to anyone's private information unless I have been given permission, and being that I had worked with Rick numerous times prior, I was immediately made privy of his true condition. I knew he needed to get another opinion and fast, as this was much more than they were initially thinking it might be. I knew with all of my soul that this dear friend of ours had cancer and was not yet aware of the fact. Rick saw me coming down the dock, knowing full well that I was overhearing the conversation, and we locked eyes. I did not verbally say one word out loud to Rick, but our souls spoke, and he simply said, *"Suz? Do you think I need to investigate this further?"* I only needed to nod my head and he knew. We both knew. And we were both right.

Rick's cancer journey did indeed completely change my life, as a healer as well as a human being. At this point I was very early in my career as an energy practitioner, and still fairly ignorant about how spirit really worked. Rick and I had made a plan to begin to do some serious healing work together on his cancer. This would obviously assist him in this medical condition, but also support me in honing my energy practitioner skills. I worked with Rick as often as possible in person. In the beginning, it was a bit difficult as he lived on the far south end of the cities and I was far north, but we did our best. We also made an effort to work together when we were both up north at our cabins. When his family was also at the cabin, we would include them in our efforts, enjoying many opportunities to learn about the chakras. I shared how the body dis-eases which can eventually turn to *disease* according to any block in the consciousness flow of that chakra. I presented the importance of alignment with truth when it comes to energy and its flow. This was an entirely new concept to the family and they began to devour the materials, trying everything they could to help their dad/husband. We would collaborate for hours on the concepts of self-healing and how it was critical to understand the chakra system to assist in finding a better balance of energy for *all of their bodies*: physically, emotionally, mentally, and spiritually. If Rick was going to get through this and learn to self-heal, they all needed to be on the same page. There was as much laughter and hope as there were tears of fear during these weeks.

I was also working with oracle angel cards daily to try to get additional messages for Rick and a funny thing started to happen with these. I found myself pulling the same two cards over and over, when out of 44 cards I continually drew the two cards that read: *Problem Resolved* and *Miracle Healing*. I began to hold real hope that this work was truly helping Rick's diagnosis and was completely taken aback one day when he called and informed me that his latest tests showed that his cancer had now spread rapidly throughout most all of his body. They informed him that his time had now become very short. It had been less than six weeks since this entire scenario began, and now they were saying he possibly only had a few weeks left.

I was devastated to say the least. In fact, I was more than that—I was incredibly angry. I clearly remember going up into my healing room where I did most of our work and throwing my oracle cards across the room as tears streamed down my face. I screamed to whatever "God" Source energy was listening at how unfair it was, and how cruel it was to have given us such messages as *Problem Resolved* and *Miracle Healing* over and over only to find that he was so much worse off now. I was incredibly frustrated to feel as if my work on Rick was a sham, not really helping him in any way. That I had failed as a healer. This was the point where my life changed forever.

At that moment, my husband Chuck walked up the stairs of my healing room and found me in this state of anger and madness as I shared Rick's current condition and how I was tricked by the oracle cards. Then, a miracle lesson happened. A calm came over Chuck's face—it was soft and filled with light, and his quiet voice simply said, *"Suzanne, what would make you think that your version of a miracle healing is the same as the one of Rick's soul?"* I know with all my heart, mind, and body that voice was not one of my actual husband. In fact, the words much less the delivery, were not that of Chuck. It truly was a Divine message that came from somewhere else, and was intended for me to hear loud and clear. It was a very important message of: *I am NOT the healer of anyone I work on or with. Source/God is the healer. I am only the channel. I have no right to project my version of healing onto anyone at any time. Their soul chooses and I need to honor that choice.* I was ashamed. I was humbled. I was grateful.

Rick's soul knew exactly what it was doing to follow the contract he had originally signed up for as an incarnation here on Earth in human form. It was not for me nor anyone else to see the way this scene was playing out as something other than Divine. It is not for me to judge that it is unfair, wrong, or horrible to have a journey that ends in death from cancer. The way this journey was playing out was the divine manifestation of his truth: *Problem Resolved* and *Miracle Healing*. I had taken those cards as literal messages seen through my own filter of ego. This cancer offered the chance to do the work to clear all karma and debt within this lifetime and move forward into Source with a clear record. The plan was revealing itself exactly the way his soul had intended and I had no business coloring it from my ignorant perspective. It was time for me to walk the talk of my teaching and help him and his family move forward with love, not fear. Loving the process of death and dying versus fearing it.

We are all going to die. This death sentence was an amazing and courageous learning opportunity for Rick and his family. Our energy lessons radically changed to view self-healing from a new perspective, one of healing the soul body and accepting death as not an ending but a transition. We talked about soul contracts and how each of them were an integral part of this partnership well beyond their third-dimensional selves. We talked about how they signed up for this journey as much as Rick had and what that meant to their own individual reason for being a part of this cancer ride. Rick dug deep into the consciousness of the chakras that affected his body to see where he was blocked in true alignment with Source, initially causing the cancer in his body. He worked tirelessly to release anger and self-worth issues that had plagued him since childhood. Rick re-examined the truth of relationships and let go of any old wounds. He found forgiveness for himself and others, knowing fully that these energy releases would ultimately make his final hours easier in terms of transition back to spirit. He performed many sacred rituals in the early mornings and the late nights to connect with the magic of the north woods, intimately uniting with nature and universe. He did so much work to ready himself and I was completely in awe of his efforts.

In the final weeks of working with Rick, it became more and more difficult to physically get together with him to perform our healings, so we began to work over the phone. Up to this point in my career as an energy worker, I had only really trusted my hands to do the work and now this offered me a chance to hone a new and amazing skill: complete telepathy. I could now tap into Rick whenever needed via intention only by using my head and heart connection. This became the new normal for my work. I continued to see him in person whenever we could make it happen, the cabin being our favorite place to connect. I distinctly remember one healing session up north where I was privileged to find an energy connection to Source that I have never again been able to replicate: working in the *Harmonics of Creation* itself. We live in layers and layers of consciousness, and that consciousness is made up of love and light.

One level of this consciousness is so very high up in existence most of us never get to experience it unless we have a *Near Death Experience* or die ourselves. This is the plane of existence in *Sound*, or the Harmonics of Creation. It is the music of Divine formation. The rubbing together of the strings of conception. It is what people describe in near death experiences as music that is *so beautiful, unlike anything they have ever heard before*. The healings I do are telepathic, and so Rick was basically resting as I went into a deep meditative state, and this is where I became one with this amazing music. It was such a gift, and I am forever grateful to have lived through this. Returning from that experience and coming back into my own physical body was very difficult, as the love quotient is so extremely high in vibration that our human form needs to shudder and shake in order to restore itself back into its balance of meat-and-bone. Rick was peacefully sleeping when I was finished, but my tears were still flowing and my voice and body still shuddering as I opened the door from our session to find his family terrified that he had left this Earth. Rick was fine, I told them, it was me that was the vibrational mess.

Another time at the cabin I was working on Rick remotely as he was too sick now to travel up to his cabin. I was on my pontoon on the water working, only to open my eyes and find three eagles circling over my head! Two Bald Eagles and one Golden. A Golden

Eagle is not typically found in our area, so this to me was a special sign. Whenever I worked on Rick, the eagles would fly. I also did a ritual for him up at the cabin that night because up north, and the fire pit, was his "Happy Place" and I knew the energy there was strong for him. It was very late and I was working at the fire long after everyone else had gone to bed, remotely connecting with Rick only to look down and find a bright shiny penny right in the middle of the fire pit. I dug it out the following day when it was cooled. It had done its job and I gifted it to Rick the next time I saw him. He used it when he meditated and kept it at his bedside. I felt he indeed was my lucky penny as the gifts he gave to me were so much more than I had offered him during these short yet intense weeks.

I was fortunate enough to be able to be with Rick and his entire family at the end of his journey in the Mayo Clinic intensive care unit. Even then this gentle giant was filled with laughter and joy. Even though his enormous AWA/WWF frame was now reduced to skin and bone—he kept his faith in Source strong. He believed in the work of his soul and I was blessed to be a first-hand witness to it all. The love in that room was palpable. The energy was something I have never again experienced to that level. I will always be grateful for those last hours in the hospital where he told the ER nurses that if he could not swallow or breathe, *he didn't want any of those stupid tubes down his throat because his healer was here and he trusted her work more than theirs*. As the hours went on and he found himself having difficulty, those very same nurses really did allow me to shift his energy first rather than opting for any invasive tubes…and it worked. How crazy it must have looked to those medical professionals to divert the work of devices to the lady in the corner quietly clutching a crystal and breathing loudly with her eyes closed. I am so grateful for them allowing me to do my work for Rick.

It was later that day when I got to experience first-hand Rick finding his true guardian angel, with him fully knowing that the presence at his side was real and true. I had intimate moments of clarity with him where we shared just how beautiful this journey was for us both. I left the family to experience his final couple hours alone, knowing fully he would peacefully die during my travels back home that night or the next day—and he did. Rick's wife Steph told me that she was sleeping in a recliner by his bed when a nurse came in and called his name. There was no response and Steph knew he was gone. The sun was just rising when the family and chaplain came in to pray. Steph looked out the window and saw a flock of birds spiraling up to the sky—she knew then that Rick was on the next part of his journey.

I will always treasure this story of Rick and his cancer because I believe it is my story, too. Because of him, I learned that I am *NOT* the healer, that we heal our Self with the help of God/Source. I learned humility. I learned to trust. I learned that we do indeed have a Higher Self that *is* in charge of this journey we call life and if we learn to surrender to this energy in love versus fear, even the experience of death itself can be amazing. I learned a person, much less a family, can choose to go through the death experience with just as much laughter, joy, and wonder as they can with grief, resentment, and sadness.

Rick was buried with a beautiful shiny penny in his hand to signify the work we all did. It took many of us to make this journey: him, his Higher Self, his Guides and Angels, his family, his friends, his medical team, and *me*. I am forever grateful to have been invited to be on this team. And Rick is still on mine, as he visits and supports me during healing sessions, often playing with my music, my lights, and more. I know his spirit is busy, entertaining a much different audience and in a much bigger ring.

Third Level Summary

- This is the beginning of letting go of all physical realities of time and physical laws.
- The dying person may physically appear to be struggling. This is the templates releasing—from an energy standpoint, it is a calm release.
- Breathing patterns may become jerky, gurgling, and unsettling to witness.

- The dying person encounters their contrasting dual power sources—the *ME* of human EGO and the *WE* of collective spirit.
- Begins mottling: feet, hands, and sometimes arms begin to turn blackish-blue and blotchy because robust energy centers or chakras are closing.
- Body has web-effect: discoloration of white-ish splotches because very light yellowish lines of auric mental energy body grid are dissolving.
- The energy in the room may be somewhat heavy.

Fourth Level of Transition

4th Dimension of Light / Heart Chakra or Bridge / Auric Astral Body
Final Release of *"all we create"* as the *MIND* of Human Form Energies

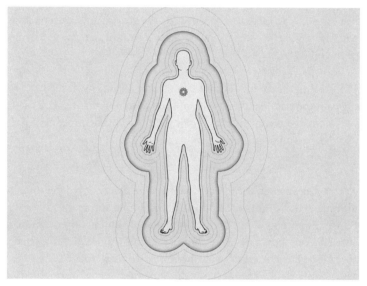

Heart Chakra and Auric Astral Body

The fourth chakra, the heart chakra, is related to all we've created as an individual human being. When this chakra is released, we are in the initial stages of sending our file of information to the Akashic Record, where it returns to spirit and becomes our Book of Life when the death experience is final. This is the:

- Final release of consciousness to send home the Akashic Record of human form.

- Final release of the mind—all conscious and unconscious thought and ideas that manifest.
- Final release from the fourth dimension of light: the collective unconscious, mental in nature.
- Shutting down and then dissolving the heart chakra.
- Shutting down and then dissolving the astral energy body.
- Crossing back over the astral plane and/or "bridge" to the spiritual plane.

For those assisting anyone through the death process, you may witness varying levels of the dying person's fear or struggle with some of the following:

- Seeing the dying person have a flurry of activity. It seems they are connecting and communicating better again. This actually means they are moving forward in their journey.
- There can be a charged feeling in the actual room of the dying person.

As our heart center, the fourth chakra emotionally embodies unconditional love. We are now working beyond time and space within the fourth dimension of light—the astral plane found within the human aura and the anchor of the soul's personality. This is where we release an experience *as a mind* of all thoughts and ideas that have worked to formulate and manifest the human body. This bridge in our energy field crosses us back over from the physical plane of the lower vibrating energy bodies and bridges upward to the spiritual plane of the higher vibrating energy bodies. At this period, I *see* the heart chakra, as well as the next three spiritual chakras, not as vortexes residing inside the human body, but as vertical images, lines, or dimensions aligning, almost floating above the physical body.

This fourth transition takes place on the astral plane. The next five transitions will take place on spiritual planes where all remaining chakras, energy bodies, and light dimensions will still need to be released before we see the human body expire. At this time, the person is releasing all they created in human form energies. They are sealing the file of information in their Akashic Record of *"all they created"* as a human form. This file of information will return to spirit and become content for the person's Book of Life. This is done by mentally releasing the fourth dimension of light.

Energetically, you can see and feel a strong shift at this time in the room and around the body as the astral plane is crossed. A beautiful, colorful energy now actually hovers above and about the human form. It moves much like a lava lamp, with playful swirls and orbs of energy floating above the individual. This can be a very confusing time for those holding vigil for the dying person. There often seems to be almost a revitalization of the body or a flurry of activity during this phase. Sometimes the person almost has a burst of energy, and this can be puzzling for those holding vigil. There is also an almost charged feeling within the room—very slight and very subtle, but electric. These confusing signals can be misinterpreted by those in attendance as a halt to the dying process. In actuality, the energy is "powering-up" to move to the next phase—the spiritual plane and *full release of humanness.*

Now more than ever, this is a time of being present for them without judgment and self-ego on our part. Those in attendance must be patient and allow the dying person the opportunity to continue their journey with the faith that they are moving forward in accordance with their own personal plan. Family members, friends, or medical attendants can give verbal or nonverbal permission to the dying person to move through this transition. Giving this permission can actually make this phase easier for the person who is dying. It is as simple as a non-judgmental gift of sharing divine love.

I often find that when the dying person has fully cleared the astral plane and is working on the spiritual planes, the hours of actual death are usually fairly short as the person continues onward. This fourth level of transition occurs as a *final release* of all human form energies as the mind of creation. It is beginning to return to oneness. As we move to the next level, we will see how we move toward the *shutting down* of universal energies in the journey to the fifth level.

What I *Psychically See* at this Level

During this time, I psychically *see* beautiful blobs and swirls of color begin to hover over, above, and around the person. The auric colors are soft swirling orbs of energy floating musically above the person and throughout the room.

Psychically, I also begin to see vertical lines or images floating above the body. This takes the place of any chakra vortexes that I previously saw within the body.

As I work to assist the person through this phase, their heart chakra, now seen as a vertical line, will go dark and then dissolve. My job is to continue to assist them in releasing any fears. Telepathically talking them through this concept helps to release any energy blocks in the human body. I also help them bring in any spiritual assistance they choose to ask for in terms of helpers, guides, and loved ones from spirit.

As they continue to release, their fourth dimension of light will dissolve as does their bridge or astral body of the aura. It is a transmuting of energy—a returning to Source.

What Your Loved One *May Be* Psychically Experiencing at this Level

The floodgates have been opened, and the energy now ramps up as the person becomes aware of the love and light supporting their energetic transition from this point forward. By now most people are beginning to notice their spirit-helpers, usually starting with their guardian angel. I find that many dying people feel their guardian is stationed at the top of the bedside, over their shoulder.

Additionally, at this phase, the dying person can also become aware of deceased loved ones entering the scene to support the journey, from spouses to parents, grandparents, and even pets. Psychically, many show themselves as simply energy signatures, much like wiggly lines of heat visible above pavement on a scorching day. Others may see a full apparition of how their loved one appeared physically during their life. It all depends on the dying person's beliefs and how they choose to bring in the information.

Healing Strategies for this Level

- Make sure you and all caregivers are getting sufficient rest, food, and fresh air.
- You may want to discuss the wants and needs of a service for your loved one. Choose a favorite poem, prayer, or picture. Determine if this conversation is better discussed in the presence of the dying person or in private with other family members.
- Share great stories and memories at bedside with your loved one, fully reassuring them that everyone will be fine and taken care of at all times.
- Celebrate their lives.
- Tell your loved one out loud or in your heart that you love them and just what they mean to you.
- Allow the room to be quiet when needed, too much activity is not good for anyone involved.

Fourth Level Case Study:
A Past Life Holds the Journey Hostage

Is there a heaven and hell? Almost all scriptures of the world talk about heaven and hell, so what exactly do they really mean by these terms? What do we really know? Do we understand their esoteric meaning and mystic suggestions, or are we merely satisfied with what we learned in grade school? Sometimes we go through our entire life believing in the spoon-fed grade school version and sometimes we still believe it even after our death.

Steve was a pretty close friend of my brother-in-law; they had known each other since early grade school days. I knew Steve at a distance, relating to him on a very limited basis at family functions or out for an evening with my sister and her husband. To me, Steve always seemed to be a socially awkward man, not terribly interested in much beyond himself and he presented a detached nature. His energy field was prickly, and to be honest, I rarely interacted with him unless I had to. Steve contracted a pretty rare form of cancer in his early 40s and began quite an extensive journey, eventually landing him in the hospital to play out his last days on earth in hospice care.

We heard numerous stories of the hospital staff encounters with Steve—most of which were not pleasant. I perceived him as a difficult man experiencing life, and it seemed he was playing out that same role in death. Ironically, a friend of mine ended up as one of his hospital staff caretakers and she, too, encountered the wrath of Steve during her shifts. He was basically rude to most of the nursing staff, the hospital grief counselors, and anyone else trying to assist, including my sister, yet she continued to make ongoing visits to him. Steve was having no part of any spiritual esoteric conversation, so my sister kept it simple, only talking about day to day activities and sharing information about his still living 80-some year-old mother. Steve was well into the point of hospice care, moving in and out of consciousness, yet he continued to hang on, day after day, week after week.

After quite some time, even the hospital staff were amazed at the tenacity of Steve's human will. His medical condition should have taken him from this world many weeks back, but he continued to fight, and they did not really know why. This is when my sister and brother-in-law asked me to assist to see if I could psychically find out what was holding Steve here and possibly aid him in moving forward. Steve was aware of the healing work that I did, but had no interest, much less belief in the concept. At this point in his journey however, he said he didn't really care one way or the other if I wanted to come visit. At least I could spend time with my sister as she was clocking many hours at his bedside, so we made a time for me to stop by.

When I entered the hospital room, the energy within was thick and dense. The aura of the room was heavy, filled with anger and fear. Steve was in and out of consciousness, his body in no way struggling, yet his aura was. It was as if all of his physical chakras—the root, sacral, and solar plexus—were all battling to release at the same time. His aura held such conflict, as if he were fighting himself through this passage. After visiting with my sister, I chose a small chair in the far corner to begin my work. As I have stated before, I move energy telepathically, so if you see me working on someone, I may simply look as though I'm in a state of quiet contemplation or prayer. Before I had even got a chance to tap into Steve's energies, the hospital chaplain entered and it was obvious by his conversation with my sister that they were previously acquainted.

I was then introduced as a healer and hospice worker in addition to knowing Steve via my sister, and the chaplain exclaimed that he hoped that my work might assist Steve. He said he was well aware of the energy struggle going on and shared how the hospital staff had concerns of how Steve continued to fight, causing ongoing exhaustion for everyone involved. He said he would check back later after his rounds, and I returned to my work.

Initially what I found in Steve's field was the ego struggle of not wanting to let go of stuff. Steve had worked for years to accumulate his world of stuff, as so many of us do. He was proud of his accomplishments, his things, and was not happy to let them go even now. I find this to be a very typical block for many going through the early stages of the death process and work to assist the person in knowing that stuff is something they can choose to let go of now, and by so doing, the transition becomes easier. It is a fear-based ego belief that for many is a difficult release, Steve included.

I remained in the hospital room for close to an hour, continuing to lend a hand in moving the energies. The chaplain did return to excitedly exclaim he could actually feel quite a difference in the overall energy of the room. He was extremely interested in how that happened and we moved into the outer hall to chat. When we were finished, I returned to tell my sister I was leaving to go back home to continue to work on Steve remotely from my office and told her I would check in later via telephone. Sometimes I can get stronger psychic information by actually working remotely on the dying person and this certainly turned out to be the case with Steve. During my remote session in my office, I kept getting the clear message that somewhere deep within the psyche of Steve, he was terrified to die because he was convinced that he was going to hell. The information never came verbally from the physical Steve—only psychically from his spirit. This message consistently came through as I continued to dig deeper on how and why that belief was so stuck within his psyche. I was then presented with an extremely clear and vivid past life movie that brought this concept into perspective. When I get past life information, sometimes it comes to me in a visual of very old movie reels, choppy yet clear distinct visions. They sometimes look like the negatives on the old photo films, each with its own picture, collectively telling the story, one frame at a time.

This particular story was one of a Civil War Confederate Soldier. I could clearly see his face—the face of another life of Steve, complete with some of the same or similar facial features, but definitely a different person in a soldier's uniform. I could distinctly see the criss-cross emblem on his uniform hat, buttons down his outfit, war attire gun slung over the shoulder, and so on. What most stood out was the enormous handlebar mustache on his face and the cold grey eyes. This was an angry man. One that even in spirit form carried fear fueled by hatred. This man had indeed died in war and carried all that hate into the beyond where he met his fate with this own version of "Hell." And for some unknown reason, this past life of Steve, complete with the fear-based belief of Hell, was intertwined in this current version of Steve and holding his death process hostage in fear. I have no knowledge if the actual Steve dreaded hell or not, but this past life solider certainly did.

For many people, the idea of past lives may seem silly and not believable, and that is OK. For me, however, I have found many past life scenarios that are aurically affecting either the physical person or the person in spirit, and I believe they can be very detrimental. In the case of Steve, it was the fear of the return to hell that was prohibiting him from clearing his chakras and allowing him to proceed as needed. I energetically worked with this "other version of Steve" to heal the hatred and release the aura and chakra blocks so that he himself could fully return to Source energy.

The most amazing part of this case was the phone call I had to my sister to tell her what I had found. She herself is incredibly intuitive and psychic, with vivid third-eye sight, and we often find ourselves comparing our findings when we do spirit work. She had remained at the hospital when I had gone to my office to do the remote work and was basically in her own meditative state of prayerful support, and lo and behold, she experienced the same Confederate Soldier I was releasing from the past life. But the incredible thing is how she saw the information—it was on the current Steve's actual face. She said for some reason she had opened her eyes only to find herself staring at a Steve with a giant handlebar mustache and a uniform on!

And remember, I had not yet even shared what I had found in the work. She said it was the craziest thing, as if a holographic projection was overlaid on the actual Steve, and without the background story, it had her totally baffled to say the least. I then revealed my findings. We shared experiences and compared notes, concluding the current Steve was most likely connected aurically to the past life one.

My sister returned home that evening to a phone call telling her that Steve had passed away quietly within the hour after she had left the hospital. That was one of the most surreal and incredible opportunities to release a hell that was not even real, and I am blessed to have been able to assist both Steves back to Source.

There is no real evidence currently to support the actual view of heaven or hell. According to esoteric tradition or Ageless Wisdom, everyone after death enters another plane or state of consciousness known as the astral plane or the astral world. To the psychic or the medium, it is simply known as the plane where we connect to gain information and do work. After the death of the physical body, our astral-emotional body or the vehicle for our emotional feeling nature and the mind, still remains. This allows us to function on the astral plane. The astral plane is an illusion created by the human mind and is very much like living in a dream where you create your own hell or heaven. It is the same plane of consciousness associated with our dreams during sleep. We co-create our lives as well as our death experience.

Quite possibly, heaven is a higher Spiritual state of consciousness, and hell is a lower state of consciousness. That sure seems to be the case with our Confederate Soldier Steve. The enlightened mind may be its own heaven whereas the unenlightened mind is its own hell.

Fourth Level Summary

- Releases all thoughts and ideas that have worked to formulate and manifest the human body.
- Bridges the physical plane to the spiritual plane.
- Can be a very confusing time for those holding vigil for the dying person.
- Seems to be almost a revitalization of the body.
- A flurry of activity or burst of energy, can be puzzling.
- There may be a charged feeling within the room.
- Confusing signals can be misinterpreted by those in attendance.
- Hours until actual death are often fairly short.

Fifth Level of Transition

5th Dimension of Light / Throat Chakra / Auric Etheric Template
Shuts down the consciousness of *"all we experience"* as the *BODY* of Universe Energies

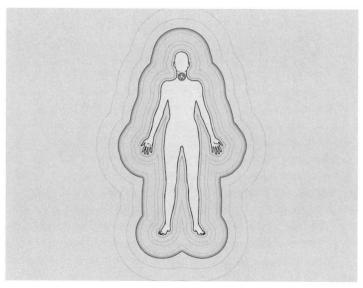

Throat Chakra and Auric Etheric Template

The fifth chakra, or throat chakra, holds our connection to the universe. When we release this chakra, we let go of our physical connection to an individual self in an *individual* consciousness and begin to move back to a *collective* consciousness. This includes:

- Shutting down consciousness of living out the experience of Universe.

- Shutting down the "You" and "I" and returning to "WE."
- Shutting down individuality, returning to the much greater awareness of group identity.
- Shutting down the fifth dimension of light: the collective consciousness, emotional in nature.
- Shutting down and then dissolving the throat chakra.
- Shutting down and then dissolving the auric etheric template energy body.

For those assisting anyone through the death process, you may witness varying levels of the dying person's fear or struggle with some of the following:

- Seeing our loved one trying to communicate to those in attendance or to those we cannot necessarily see.
- Seeing our loved one reach out to someone that you physically may not see in the room, such as angels, guides, or passed loved ones.
- Seeing our loved one react positively or negatively to the sounds throughout the room, for example to levels of music or people in attendance. Try to keep the room calm.

As our throat center, the fifth chakra is where the power of the word and our communication energy resides. The energy body is the auric etheric template and first level of the spiritual plane where we are working to release an experience *as a body* of the universe energies. This transition resides in the fifth dimension of light, the dimension of unity where the dying person is letting go of all *individual* consciousness and harmoniously merging back to a *collective* consciousness.

At this time, even when our loved one may be directly unresponsive, we can find their eyes sometimes opening and searching. We find them talking or mouthing words, looking or reaching out to someone in the room who is not there to our physical eyes. Because the dying process is now playing out in the spiritual plane, spirit-helpers begin to arrive to assist the person. Family, friends, and medical staff may not be able to see or even be aware of this energetic assistance, but our loved one is. This can be experienced as either confusing or comforting depending on belief systems. These vibrational beings will slowly move closer and closer to the dying person's body-energy as they progress through the next stages.

At this period, spirit-helpers usually stay a bit back from the person and float in the corners of the room or along far walls. The heavenly light of Source dimly begins to align from the far corner of the dying person's room. This light is where we initially came from and where the person in the process of dying is now aligning to return to. This light is Source, or God. At this time, the energetic light shines a bit dim as planes are still aligning, but it is definitely visible to the psychic eye. That is why we often hear our loved ones claim to see the light. They do. There is also a distinct horizontal pathway of the dimensions left that begins to lead toward the light. This path connects the vertical lines or veils that float above the body and represent the remaining individual light dimensions, chakras, and energy bodies yet to be crossed along the spiritual plane. At this time, those in attendance can see the person's physical body seem to almost die and yet come back again. Often, they seem to stop breathing only to start up again. This flip-flop happens as the energies shift back and forth from individual energies to collective energies releasing the *I* versus the *We* of this transition.

The throat chakra is all about the divine voice, and so it is a time to be present for our loved one by verbalizing our feelings to them. We can do this either out loud, in our minds, or in our hearts. It is a time to communicate our messages of divine love to and for our loved one as he or she continues to transition in energy. It is also a time to verbally or mentally communicate messages outward to those that may assist them in their journey, whether it is a relative or friend in spirit, or angels and spirit guides. Do not be afraid to ask for spirit-based assistance from Source energy. Any family member, friend, or medical attendant can be there physically, emotionally, mentally, and spiritually for the dying person in this manner.

At this time, the person is releasing their individuality and returning to collectivity and unity of consciousness. They are letting go of their power of the word. Oftentimes here we will find them whispering or their mouths may be silently moving as they speak without words to others we cannot see. They are remembering how to communicate without the voice, utilizing telepathy and love-based communication. The energy of *"all they experienced"* as this consciousness will now transform into an energetic file of information for their Akashic Record for the experience of being a universe form.

This energetic file of information will return to spirit and become content for the person's Book of Life. This fifth level of transition occurs to *shut down* all universe energies as the body of experience. As we move to the next level, we will see how these same universal energies transition as a *final release* in their journey to the sixth level.

What I *Psychically See* at this Level

During this time, I psychically *see* beautiful etheric beings beginning to come into the person's room. At this time, these beings usually are staying around the perimeter of the room, hovering in the corners.

Psychically, I also begin to see heavenly white light of Source, dimly beginning to align from the far corner of the dying person's room. This directly corresponds to the path of the vertical lines of energy that represent the person's chakras still working to dissolve.

As I work to assist the person through this phase, their throat chakra is now seen as a vertical line. It will go dark and then dissolve, moving the entire pathway closer to the light.

I also can now begin to see them communicate with the spiritual helpers in the room, as they reach out and whisper in communication to them. I can sometimes hear them communicating with their guides and helpers, because at this point we no longer need our human voice.

By now, I usually am aware of their personal Guardian Angel, oftentimes standing at the left shoulder of the person.

As they continue to release their fifth dimension of light and throat chakra, their etheric template of the aura dissolves. It is a transmuting of energy—a returning to Source.

What Your Loved One *May Be* Psychically Experiencing at this Level

Because this is the communication chakra, the dying person remembers their knowing of telepathic conversing, and this offers a new sense of joyous return to family. Your loved one's Higher Self begins to take the lead in connecting with the incoming energies of love and support from guides, angels, and loved ones who begin to manifest with more detail. This is why we see the dying person act as if they are speaking with someone who we think isn't necessarily there, but indeed they are—from an energetic perspective. This connection may be strong or weak, depending on the belief system of the person.

For me, this fifth level of transition also offers the initial awareness of the white light and the path towards it. Many people find themselves in awe during this phase and may make verbal reference to it.

Healing Strategies for this Level

- Make sure you and all caregivers are getting sufficient rest, food, and fresh air.
- If the time is appropriate, begin to allow your loved one to go, to move onward, and let them return to Source. Oftentimes they need our permission.
- If this is the case, tell them that all those who are left behind will be just fine and reassure the person that all things will be taken care of for them.
- Begin to let go yourself and try not to control the situation. Honor the journey and the soul contract of your loved one by not holding them back.
- Express your thoughts and feelings with your loved one, either out loud or in your heart.

97

Fifth Level Case Study:
Alzheimer's and the Soul

When I do hospice work, it is usually with those patients who are non-responsive and in need of vigil only. I normally do not visit and work with those who are still here interacting verbally in the 3-D world.

One day while out with another hospice co-worker, I joined her on a visit to one of her patients who was in a nursing home Alzheimer's ward. He was an immigrant named Klaus, in his early 70s, and he had full blown Alzheimer's. He basically was not able to interact at all—and had not spoken a word to anyone in over three years at the nursing home. He was unshaven and had his lunch still somewhat on his sweater. His hair was long and out of sorts, laid disheveled about his head. His eyes were blank and he made no indication that he even realized or cared we were in his presence. While my co-worker was chatting away with Klaus, I began scanning his bookshelves and the walls of his room. To my surprise—he had many books on spiritualism and metaphysics and several photos with him in younger years with monks and holy men in India. At first glance, I never would have guessed he was so interested in this material, but his collection told another story.

I speak telepathically to most all my non-responsive patients and Klaus was immediately surprised that he could indeed "hear me" talking to him in my mind. He said something along the lines of *"Hey how can you hear me?"* And I said, *"Well, how can YOU hear ME?"* And he laughed inside. While my friend was physically chatting away with him, I was telepathically chatting up my own conversation with Klaus. I had no knowledge of this man in any manner, and yet through this short chat, he told me that he was very sad and lonely because his friend Shannon no longer came to visit. I relayed this to my co-worker whose case it was, and to her surprise, she was a bit confused that I somehow knew his ex's name that had indeed been on file. Shannon had moved away and no longer came to visit as of a couple years ago. I continued my silent conversation with Klaus and gained additional insight into his past. It was funny because he was questioning me as much as I was him and so it went, but he was still completely nonresponsive verbally and physically.

At one point I had said, in a totally sarcastic humor, that I bet at one time in his life he had been pretty hot, but that was well before he allowed his lunch to reside on his sweater and his hair to go awry. He physically lurched forward in his wheelchair, belted out a verbal belly laugh, flew his head in my direction to make full eye contact as he waved his hands about. I thought my co-worker was going to fall off her chair. Our communication had been telepathic, so all my co-worker heard was an outburst out of the blue. Klaus and I were laughing and she was stunned.

After a bit, we calmed down once again to have a more serious conversation now that the communication energy was flowing between us. I was curious as to what he was experiencing in traversing the death experience of Alzheimer's disease. I asked him why, if he was not in body, did he choose to continue being here at all. I asked what he did when he was gone, or not in there, in his human shell per se. He informed me that when gone, he was actually traversing multi-dimensionally. That his soul was truly out there working in other places, times, and universus beyond what we know as 3-D. And in between those work efforts is when he would indeed come back in his human body for a bit. That this human form was essentially the break from the work, in a manner of speaking.

I asked him why he did not simply choose to move onward then and do that other work fully, why his human form was still in existence here in what we see as an extremely unfulfilling life form. He simply stated that he was not done holding the light. He explained that our human body holds light for this planet and universe and that the human form is the way that we do that. Only when it is time does that job stop, he said. That was an extremely enlightening conversation to say the least. I never again saw the disease or Alzheimer's the same after that day.

I continued to visit Klaus over the next couple of months any time I was at that nursing home location and he was always excited to see me. The staff was very confused in the way his body reacted when I arrived, as he was animated, excited, and verbal—something he never did at any other time while there. It was a quandary to them all, our little secret! I was not with him the day he died, however I know he was indeed ready and knew full well it was now the time to fully go. He was an amazing experience and I am honored to have known him.

Fifth Level Summary

- The dying person can be directly unresponsive and/or can flip flop from conscious to unconscious.
- There is a letting go of all individual consciousness.
- They harmoniously merge back to a collective consciousness.
- Their eyes are sometimes opening and searching.
- Spirit-helpers begin to arrive to assist the person.
- There may be talking, looking, or reaching at someone in the room that is not there to our physical eyes.
- Breathing stops only to start up again.

Sixth Level of Transition

6th Dimension of Light / The Third-Eye Chakra or Brow / Auric Celestial Body
Final Release of *"all we create"* as the MIND of Universe Energies

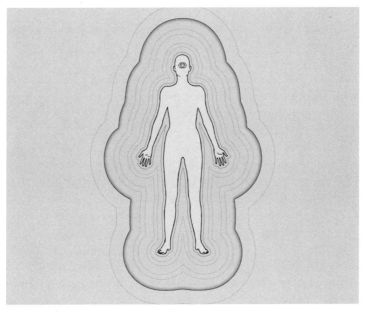

Third-Eye Chakra and Auric Celestial Body

The sixth chakra connects us to the universal building blocks that allow us to co-create. When we release this chakra, we are letting go of our ability to co-create in this life as a human expression and experience. Beyond this dimension, there is no structure or form and all things simply become Source.

It is the:

- Final release of consciousness to send home the final Akashic Record of Universe.
- Final release of the language of life and light of all things manifest.
- Final release of the study of form and structure where ideas took shape.
- Final release of the sixth dimension of light: realm of sacred geometry, the collective *un*consciousness, mental in nature.
- Shutting down and then dissolving the third-eye chakra.
- Shutting down and then dissolving the auric celestial energy body.

For those assisting anyone through the death process, you may witness varying levels of the dying person's fear or struggle with some of the following:

- At this stage, the person often takes on an opaque-like essence and there may be a glow surrounding their body.
- The room itself begins to vibrate at a higher level. If you can calm yourself enough to recognize this, it is a beautiful time.
- This is sometimes when the dying person tries to convey any last messages to their loved ones.

The sixth chakra is our third-eye center. This chakra is trust and clarity on an intuitive level. The auric field is the celestial body which is a range of love that extends beyond anything a human can know and encompass in life. We are working to release an experience *as a mind* of the sixth dimension of light, the realm of sacred geometry. The person is releasing their language of life and light from which all things have become manifest.

This is letting go of knowledge regarding the study of form and structure now intuitively embracing its truth of returning home, returning to Source or God. This is the time we often see a soft glow emanate from the person's face and body. It is as if the entire room takes on an opaque or pearly-soft look. It is a beautiful time to find peace, joy, and love on your loved one's face and body if you are able. It is an opportunity to see the miracle of this process. There is calm to both the dying person and the energy of the room. The first vertical veil on the horizontal pathway toward the "light" will eventually dissipate, allowing the incoming light of Source to become a bit stronger. Both the third-eye chakra and the celestial energy body are moving toward a vibration of intuition and consciousness as well as releasing form and space.

We are at the point in the journey where any family member, friend, or medical attendant's presence is there to simply hold space in divine love and support the death process. It is a time of reverence and respect for not only the journey, but the contract the person is playing out. It is a time to honor the experience, the energy, and the loved one.

The details of that soul contract formulate the Akashic Record which is moving the energetic file of information of *"all they created"* for their universe experience back home to spirit where it will become content for the person's Book of Life. The spirit-helper energies that are in the room now move forward to support the journey onward. They are much stronger in vibration and light. They begin to place themselves closer now as they surround the dying person, starting at the head and foot of the bed and eventually filling in at the sides. Most often I find the actual Guardian Angel at the head of the bed; they are usually one of the first entities to arrive to support the process. The vibration of spirit-helpers and passed loved ones will rapidly continue to increase until they actually become a strong glow of bright yellow, gold, and white light. This is a wondrous opportunity for anyone holding vigil to experience the miracle of this process if they can allow themselves to merge with the energies of the room fully. This sixth level of transition occurs as a *final release* of all universe energies as the mind of creation. As we move to the next level, we will see how we move toward the *shutdown* of celestial soul energies in their journey to the seventh level.

What I *Psychically See* at this Level

During this time, I psychically *see* the entire room and surroundings take on an opaque or pearly-soft look. I also see the white light actually begin to make itself known in the upper corner of the room. The spiritual helpers gain in vibration and energetically begin to move closer to the side of the bed or surround the person. They place themselves at the head and foot of the bed, eventually filling in all the sides. I see them as gold and white light beings. I also can sense who they are and what they have to say, so I work to assist the person through this phase of communication. Their third-eye chakra, now seen as one of the last vertical lines, will go dark and then dissolve, moving the entire pathway even closer to the light.

This usually is a fast-paced phase, as they continue to release their sixth dimension of light and third-eye chakra to dissolve their celestial body of the aura. It is a transmuting of energy—a returning to Source.

What Your Loved One *May Be* Psychically Experiencing at this Level

The dying person's psychic self has fully kicked in at the sixth level as they now intuitively embrace their truth of returning home and aligning with Source or God. They also have full awareness of the benevolent help that surrounds them and know that they can call upon more helpers if they choose.

As the person becomes more aware, their co-creation moves into high gear to forge their path back home and the white light now becomes more defined. When the person begins energetically to enter the white light that holds their Akashic Record, this is what we might recognize as the feeling or sensation of moving through a tunnel back to Source. From a psychic standpoint, this tunnel is the etheric silver cord or tentacle of energy that connects the human incarnation to the soul-self from conception through final death. The consciousness is now working in a curious, calm, mindful state of bliss-filled surrender.

Healing Strategies for this Level

- Make sure you and all caregivers are getting sufficient rest, food, and fresh air.
- Continue to let go yourself and try not to control the situation. Honor the journey and the soul contract of your loved one.
- Try your best to allow yourself some quality meditative time with your loved one and the room itself to see if you can connect to the guidance entering at this stage.
- Allow yourself to fully grieve but also try your best to find gratitude for participating in this process.
- Pray, sing, spend these last hours in the manner your loved one would appreciate.
- Express your thoughts and feelings with your loved one, either out loud or in your heart.

Sixth Level Case Study: Rose-Infused Chakras

Oftentimes the hospice organization calls me in when a person should be further along in the death process and they are not sure as to why this is not happening. Medically speaking, the person should have died, and yet they continue to remain alive without any rational medical reason why. Ronald was one of these cases.

Ronald was an older gentleman somewhere in his 80s that had been in a nursing home for quite some time with cancer throughout his entire system. When I met him, he had been on hospice for several weeks. He specifically asked for me to come work with him to find some personal clarity as to why he was still here, when medically speaking, there was no way he should have been. He had only been surviving on liquids, water, and juice for months. He was no longer on much medicine either, and yet he experienced no pain in his physical body from his full-blown cancer. He was a bit of a medical miracle to say the least.

During my first visit with Ronald, I found him sleeping peacefully in his lounge chair in the nursing home. Not wanting to wake him from his slumber, I quietly scanned his chakras and was immediately surprised to find his aura holding a fully rose-infused light throughout his system. This indicates a very high caliber of spiritual gifts, balance, knowledge, and wisdom aligned with universal truths. I found myself extremely interested in learning more about this seemingly *normal, common, regular* older gentleman. I decided to return the following day hoping he would then be awake.

On my second visit, Ronald was indeed awake and the first thing he asked me was: *"How did my chakras look?"* I was stunned to hear a man in his eighties ask that question. This was going to be an interesting conversation, I thought. He said he wanted to know why he was still here. He knew medically there was no logical reason his body was maintaining life, and yet here he was and he wanted some answers. He felt I could give them to him. He told me that he had begun a journey of his soul in his later years in life, and that he would ask questions of his Higher Self and get his answers using a pendulum. His pendulum consisted of a button tied to the end of some yarn that originally came from a sweater he had once owned. He claimed to have used this tool for several years and had filled volumes of notebooks with information channeled from his Higher Self in terms of his past lives. He could not, however, figure out why he was still here and this is where I came into play. He knew he had "things to do" on the other side of the veil, and yet he did not understand the timeline he was being given in regard to leaving this plane of existence.

Together we did some deep healing work and I connected with his Higher Self. We learned that he was still here to gain additional knowledge. That his Higher Self and his benevolent beings who were guiding him wanted him to be at a certain level of knowledge before he crossed over. That this knowledge included his work on obtaining his past-life information and more. And that some of the work we were to do together would prepare him for his crossing at a vibrational level that was critical to his next journey of soul.

We spoke a lot about his rose-infused chakras and how that indicated the depth of his spirit knowledge, and how together we could increase that vibration even higher to assist him in a peaceful death. I shared with him how amazed I was that he could exist without any physical pain because of this divine energy throughout his fields. He indeed was a medical miracle. I worked weekly with Ronald for about three months and I have never enjoyed conversations more! The depth of his spiritual insight often left me speechless. I gifted him a beautiful crystal pendulum for his continued work. He was so excited, he used it daily.

There was such a sad side to this story, and that was Ronald's immediate family and their belief systems. I am not here to change anyone's beliefs—I can only hold my own as my truth. People get to believe whatever they choose; but in Ronald's case, this struggle was a sad part to this story. Initially, he had raised his family in the Lutheran Church. Then as time went on, he found himself expanding his beliefs and self-learning to remember what he indeed already knew inside of his soul. His self-journey of the past lives allowed his ego mind to expand into his divine mind and this scared most of his immediate family members. It did not match the dogmatic religion they had grown up with and they began to shun him and his practices. They decided that he was delusional and put him in a nursing home rather than leaving him in his own home. They made light of his past-life journals and I was told that one of his children burned them all because they considered them evil. This broke Ronald's heart.

Most all of his family were partially estranged from him, except for one adult son. I met this son one day at the nursing home when he had brought his own family for a visit with grandpa. The experience is one I will never forget. Although it was an Open House day at the nursing home, I was surprised to find members of his family there in his room. When they met me, one family member sarcastically commented that I must be that one who believed in their father's stories. I found them to be an extremely judgmental group, professing that Ronald made up ridiculous non-truths and that I had no business fueling them. They belittled him right there in front of my eyes. It was awful. Their condescending jabs at Ronald throughout this very short meeting were heartbreaking. The son and his family seemed proud of burning his journals. It was all I could do to keep professional, so I decided to leave and see him the following day. We talked then about how difficult his death process was because of these dogmatic differences in the concept of Source energy. This left him very sad and lonely, so I am glad to have befriended him when I did and to have been able to assist him in our common truths of this death/life experience.

I was going to be gone for the next two weeks because I go to Peru each January to lead a Spiritual Tour for my clients. This meant I would not be able to visit, so I told Ronald that if he chose to die while I was gone, that was OK, and that I would have him along for the trip one way or another. He laughed and claimed he was determined to stay alive until I returned two weeks later just to hear the stories because he never got to Machu Picchu in person. Sure enough, upon my return, I came to the Home to find Ronald still alive, but very much closer to death, finally. He was almost non-responsive, but when I arrived, he perked up to hear all the crazy stories of the trip. He laughed and giggled like a child, living through my experiences. It was a joy to see him again. That day when I left, I kissed his head knowing fully that I might not see him again.

The following day I got the call that he was in the final stages of dying and I went to see him. He was non-responsive at this point, but telepathically we connected. I barely had anything to shift because he was so fully aligned in his spiritual truths. His body was completely ready, as was his soul. I only worked for about 20 minutes and he peacefully died that next morning.

I know in my heart that Ronald's crossing was one of the easiest ever because his body was in direct alignment with his soul. His human experience was one of spiritual searching for truths—his own truths, not those of his family, nor anyone else's.

Sadly, his family decided to not even offer him a service for his passing but I had already said my final good-bye. He comes to visit me in spirit often anyhow. I just hope that the day his family meets him beyond the veil, they finally understand the magnitude of the soul they got to call Father and finally see him for what he truly was. I am forever grateful I got that opportunity!

Sixth Level Summary

- Releasing language of life, light, and the knowledge of form and structure.
- There may be a soft glow emanating from the dying person's face and body.

Seventh Level of Transition

7th Dimension of Light / Crown Chakra / Auric Ketheric Template
Final Release of *"all we experience"* as the *BODY* of Celestial Soul Energies

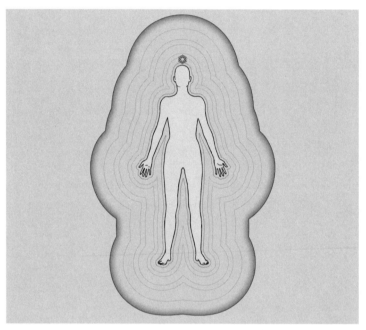

Crown Chakra and Auric Ketheric Template

The seventh and final chakra, our crown, connects us to our Higher Self. When we release this chakra, it is the final letting go of all physical shape and form in this existence. We are now moving all the life information into the Akashic Record or Book of Life to become a final file of information for the entire co-creation of this life experience.

This includes:

- Shutting down consciousness of living out the experience as a celestial soul.
- Shutting down the harmonics of creation: the planetary sounds and the galaxy.
- Shutting down all shape or form and *returning* to the abstract, less easily described in human language.
- Shutting down the seventh dimension of light: realm of cosmic sound and the collective consciousness, emotional in nature.
- Shutting down and then dissolving the crown chakra.
- Shutting down and then dissolving the auric ketheric energy body.

For those assisting anyone through the death process, you may witness varying levels of the following:

- This stage is usually very quick, moving from the last transition through this one to the next, as the spiritual helpers are hard at work now.
- Usually, the person is in a very calm state of being, and the room is vibrating higher now in love and light.

The seventh and final chakra is our crown, our Higher Self-knowingness and integration into the whole as we work in the experience of the body of the celestial soul. The crown chakra and the auric ketheric body are associated with our higher mind. We now release an experience *as a body* of all shape and form. Here, things become more abstract and less easily described in human language. The energy resides in the seventh dimension of light, which is the realm of cosmic sound, where we now release the harmonics of creation. The next horizontal veil will now begin to disappear, allowing the incoming light of Source or *home* to become stronger as the last template holding the energies of the human body together dissolve.

At this time, the person is releasing their life's pattern, moving away from all physical knowingness and toward integration of whole of Source consciousness. The energy of *"all they experienced"* in spirit will transform into an energetic file of information for their final Akashic Record for the experience of celestial soul. This energetic file of information will return to spirit and become content for the person's Book of Life. At this time, the room and dying person remain in a very calm state and the spirit-helpers become brighter and stronger.

Again, any family member, friend, or medical attendant's presence is there to simply hold space in divine love and support the death process. It is a time of reverence and respect for not only the journey, but the contract the person is playing out. It is also a time to be grateful for the entire energetic experience throughout the room or space, as you can know that spirit is indeed hard at work. Remember, if you are present, you are meant to be present. If you are not present, your loved one's spirit is still omnipresent and at work with you in any place you reside during this time.

What I *Psychically See* at this Level

During this time, I psychically *see* the spirit-helpers grow even stronger now in vibration as their glow of bright yellow, gold, and white light becomes more vibrant and more unified. The frequency of the energy within the room amplifies.

As I work to assist the person through this phase, their crown chakra, now seen as the very last vertical line, will be the last to go dark and then dissolve, moving the entire pathway closer to the light.

Psychically I continue to see the white light merge closer with the person. As they continue to release, their seventh dimension/crown chakra of light dissolves their ketheric template of the aura. It is a transmuting of energy—a returning to Source.

What Your Loved One *May Be* Psychically Experiencing at this Level

Even though the physical human body is still in transition, the psychic energetic body traversus further into the tunnel to examine the properties of their Akashic Record, either to fully surrender to the return of Source, or not. In a near death experience (NDE), this is when the person chooses to return to their human body reality, most likely because they examined their Record and determined they still have work to do. Those in alignment with the "Return to Source" energetic file will continue onward through the tunnel.

Healing Strategies for this Level

- Make sure you and all caregivers are getting sufficient rest, food, and fresh air.
- Continual gratitude is key now, being grateful for this experience of transition.
- Try to keep the situation reverent as the journey is coming to an end soon.
- Continue to journal all experiences as you will cherish these moments in months and years to come.
- Express your thoughts and feelings with your loved one, either out loud or in your heart.

Seventh Level Case Study: A Phone Conversation with a Woman about Her Death

Sometimes I have the opportunity to verbally speak to a hospice patient about their death journey, either in person or by phone. These kinds of conversations are not usually a comfortable one for most friends or family members of the dying person, and so sometimes it helps that a hospice worker can have that honest and blunt talk with them.

I was called by a client to see if I could connect with her dying Aunt Mary who was nearing the end of her journey of not only 4th stage heart disease, but also 4th stage cancer. Pretty much her entire system was shut down, yet she was still here on the physical plane and was becoming very discouraged about the idea of still being here.

These phone calls are usually a bit awkward at the beginning as how to get to the meat of the problem without sounding disconnected or uncaring of their situation. As I dialed Mary on my cell, a wave of that trepidation did hit, but by the time I heard introductory words coming out of my mouth, I knew that spirit was guiding me in what to say and do. I found myself speaking very directly with Mary about the concept of her impending death.

During the conversation, I found her to be very exhausted and tired, but willing to talk. She explained how she was sick of this fight and wished she were dead because she already felt dead and trapped here by her body. After I learned a bit of her history, I asked if she did much in the way of connecting to her Higher Self or her God-self with regard to this time in her journey. My interpretation of her answer was that she was navigating this journey mostly from a 3-D perspective, not really inviting any concept of she "gets to die." She felt forced. She felt she had no control. She felt it was happening *to her*. I eventually asked Mary if she was indeed ready to die, and she relayed to me that she was scared to leave her children. This is a very common thread for many, and as stated earlier in this book, this makes for a more difficult shut down of the affected chakra (in this case sacral), therefore extending the death process and ultimately creating unfounded fear for the person.

I asked if I could tap into her children psychically, and with her approval I shared that I felt she was estranged from the youngest daughter. Mary confirmed this as true and explained she had been gone from her life for quite some time. I kept getting the number "8" in my mind, so I asked if that number resonated for her in any way with regard to the daughter. She confirmed that was probably the age she was when she was last with her. This particular daughter was adopted, and for some reason, returned to the birth parent many years ago. The daughter was now closer to age 32 and in another part of the country where Mary had no knowledge of her or the life she had created. Mary confirmed that this daughter was the one she was referring to when she said she was scared to leave her children. Funny how the human mind works sometimes.

I explained the concept of omnipresence of spirit, and of how when we die, we transform back to full spirit. We are then an energetic signature, and she could indeed be with her daughter in a way that would be far beyond what she experienced here as detached and estranged in physical form. Mary seemed to somewhat accept that concept and we moved on in our conversation. We spoke about the idea of consciousness. It was another new concept for her to wrap her head around. I explained how the chakra system fuels our consciousness, and when this energy is not flowing in alignment with our Higher Self, it affects the physical meat-body to the extent of creating disease. I shared the levels of consciousness that were manifesting as cancer with her at this time and she claimed it actually made a lot of sense as to why these areas of her body-system had shut down. Most of Mary's disease manifestation was created by dis-ease within the heart chakra that holds the consciousness of "unconditional love."

Most every human being struggles with this idea, as we are all programmed from an early age in "conditional" love: *"I will love you if you..."*, *"I am lovable if I..."*, *"I am NOT lovable because you didn't..."* and so on. We also look to other humans to fill our love fuel-tank, rather than understanding that it is up to *us* to do this filling process ourselves. And also that we can become love-filled with fuel from so many simple pleasures, such as the wind, a flower, or a beautiful song instead of consistently needing love from another human being. Instead we fight daily for acceptance, and demand love in so many inauthentic ways that our human heart takes a beating (no pun here) as we can see by the astronomical amounts of folks struggling with heart and circulation issues, breast and lung cancer, and more.

I tried my best to get Mary to talk more about her feeling of "dead inside" and what that actually felt like. She communicated feelings of "cut off" and "all alone" even though she did have family supporting her. We talked about trying to connect to spirit more and I asked her to share with me her vision of her "God-package." She told me that it was pretty old school, even though she was only in her late fifties. God was a *He* and He was separate from her. I offered the concept of a God-package of the I AM presence of complete love energy instead, one that she was in CO-creation with. And if co-creation existed, this scenario of cancer was one that she had directly aligned with and quite possibly one of the experiences she came to have on this Earth in the first place. This was a very new and elusive concept for her to ponder in such a weakened state, but she hung in there in conversation and tried her best to listen to the possibilities of something different. I put in plain words the "soul contract" information and how her children had already signed on to be a part of this process with her, and that in and of itself gave credence to the fact that they could be OK with her gone. This gave Mary a new source of hope.

We talked about how she had every right to ask her Source energy to take her now. This idea really threw her mind into a bit of a tizzy, as she never thought she could even talk to God, much less ask Him to do something. I again reiterated that she was *of* Source, therefore completely in charge of that asking and receiving.

All of this information was new to her, and because she was very tired already, we made our conversation fairly short. Mary said she had a lot of new things to think about.

As a healer, I am never here to change anyone's belief systems. I have no right to do so. I can only offer a new perspective, a different way of owning your power from a Higher Source, and it is always the person that gets to choose to believe in their own version of truth.

I know that some of these new ideas helped Mary find peace that day, especially when it came to her estranged daughter. I don't always get to know how a person's journey ends, I can only support them in the creation of their transition.

Seventh Level Summary
- Now releases ALL shape and form.
- Releases all harmonics of creation itself.
- The dying person moves from the sixth level quickly and uneventfully through the seventh level.

Eighth Level of Transition

Final Release of *"all we create"* as the *MIND* of Celestial Soul Energies

At this point, all chakras and auric fields have shut down and we are now working in a dimension beyond shape and form. It is here we encounter the Source as divine light permeating all dimensions. We finalize and seal the Akashic Record so it now can fully return all that information back to Source.

This is the:

- Final release of consciousness to send home the final Akashic Record of celestial soul back to Source.
- Final release from eighth dimension of light: realm of divine mind, mental in nature.
- No chakras remain.
- No auric energy bodies remain.

We are working in the eighth dimension of light that is beyond shape and form as we know it. This dimension resides as the realm of the divine mind. We can only envision this dimension as the galactic Source of divine light that permeates all dimensions. No chakras or auric energy bodies of human fields remain, only spirit energy moving through light dimensions. The next vertical veil will eventually disappear as this eighth dimension energy dissipates, now allowing the incoming Source light to become very strong. At this time, the physical body of the person has most likely taken its last human breath, and is energetically returning home.

However, their spirit is still at work. Even though the person has physically expired, their spiritual energies remain in the room and are still very strong and working to release. This can be a very calm and peaceful feeling, a settling of energy. Sadly, those holding vigil are oftentimes so emotional at the loss, they miss the opportunity to experience this spiritual tranquility.

The remaining veils of light or dimensions continue to move very quickly now to release the last stages of the person's consciousness. Their energies are still transmuting as they collect their last file for their Akashic Record—one of *"all they created"* for their celestial soul experience. Their consciousness essence is calm and still present, even though their physical body has expired. The Akashic file of their entire life experience is completely sealed. It now begins to fully return to Source to finalize the content of the person's soul Book of Life.

This energetic file is what we often hear described as the movie or reel of life experiences when someone has a near death experience. In a full death experience, the file is energetically sealed, saved, and sent back to the full Akashic Library of Source.

The place where this energetic Book of Life file has been housed is what is known as the tunnel we often hear about. The light at the end of this tunnel is indeed the Source of God energies that are returning this information file home, as well as the fully energetic consciousness of our loved one.

Divine love from those in attendance at this time continues to support the death process for the person. Knowing that spirit and consciousness are still present can be a very magical time to experience the miracle of the death process.

What I *Psychically See* at this Level

During this time, I psychically *see* the continuation of the spirit-helpers working and the white light merging closer with the person. It is a transmuting of energy—a returning to Source.

What Your Loved One *May Be* Psychically Experiencing at this Level

Now the human body has expired from a 3-D standpoint, but the person's energy body and spirit guides are still at work. The person is now deep into their white-light tunnel psychic experience and has fully surrendered to aligning with Source. The guides, loved ones, angels, and benevolent beings will also now merge into the white-light tunnel to accompany the person. The white light continues to expand until it fully transmutes all energies into one, while at the same time fills the person's room with love-light energy for anyone in attendance.

During this stage, the omnipresence of the transmuting soul is now fully able to connect with whomever he or she chooses in any time/space continuum. This is why so many have a sense of the time and date a loved one dies, even from afar.

Healing Strategies for this Level

- This is probably the most difficult stage to concentrate on any sense of awe or wonder, as the person has most likely just taken their last physical breath and is now what we would call clinically dead. Most holding vigil are so emotionally frightened, sad, or angry, that they understandably miss the opportunity to see Spirit at work during this phase. Sometimes, at a later time, we can recount the experience and many spiritual moments can be remembered.
- Yes, tears and emotions are a normal part of this phase, so honor what it is that your body needs to do to experience this without judgment of self or others.
- Stay in the room, leave the room, or go back and forth—find what works for you during this time as your loved one is still transitioning aurically and throughout the room.
- Do not rush this time. Be patient with your grief, allowing yourself time and space.

Eighth Level Case Study

There are no Case Studies for the last two levels of transition because as an energy healer, my work is "done" at the seventh level of release. All human chakras have been closed, the consciousness fuel is cut off, and the auric templates are fully dissipated and released back to

Source. Energetically speaking, my work as a healer is finished just prior to these levels of release.

Eighth Level Summary

- Physical body of the person has most likely taken its last human breath.
- Spirit is still at work to move to and through the next level.
- Next levels of movement are combined and very quick.

Ninth Level of Transition

Final Release of *"all we create"* and experience as the *MIND* and the *BODY*

This is the final and full release of all transitions of level 9, including previous levels 1-8. The Akashic Record is now finalized, sealed, and returned back to Source. This is the:

- *FULL* release from the ninth dimension of light and beyond.
- No chakras remain.
- No auric energy bodies remain.
- Re-connects and *BECOMES* once again the foundation of "all we know" which includes "all we create" and "all we experience" along the journey of the life incarnation.
- Reconnects and *BECOMES* once again the consciousness of creation.
- Becomes *FULL WE*-Source consciousness.
- Returns home with all *FINAL* and sealed Akashic Records and recorded Book of Life.

Anything residing in the ninth dimension and above is technically infinite love and light residing in *all dimensions and beyond*. It is all encompassing. It is Source-God. As each vertical veil of the dimensions fade, the person is in the state of *crossing over into the light*. They are going home to Source, or God. This energy shift happens very quickly and smoothly.

I sometimes feel a very slight and subtle sensation of movement when the spirit crosses. It feels like rolling over a smooth but distinct bump in the road, filled with love and joy. There is a slight up, over, and down feeling of sorts. All energies that created the connection are now dissolved and return homeward. Sometimes when a spirit crosses at this very point, my own physical body is overwhelmed with an incredible sensation of love that causes me to actually shed tears of joy.

At this time, the person has fully released, and the energy of "all they experienced" moves fully back through their file to Source.

All energies have now released and dissolved from the human body and aura. They have fully returned to spirit. Once that release is complete, all individual chakra records combine to formulate one final Akashic Record of that overall human experience.

This is filed as their Book of Life. The good, the bad, the ugly, the exceptional, the extraordinary—it is all there, infinite and filed in energy for eternity. The person's room will still retain spirit energy for quite some time. That is why family members may find comfort in remaining by and continuing to hold vigil for their loved one directly following their experience. They oftentimes will say they intuitively know when the spirit of their loved one has passed on just by the way the overall experience feels.

What I *Psychically See* at this Level

During this time, I psychically *see* the final stages of the Spirit-helpers and the white light fully merging with the person. It is the final steps of the transmuting of human energy fully returning to Source energy.

I also can feel the celestial soul energy of the person moving into the light, and crossing over. It is a subtle yet deep knowing they moved beyond the veil. My own body has felt the love and support of the light plus those that greet the soul while crossing, and this feels like such an abundance of joy and love it is sometimes overwhelming. It is an honor to be allowed to witness this miracle of transmutation back to Source.

Edgar Cayce's *Origin and Destiny of Man* states: "All souls were created in the beginning, and are finding their way back to whence they came." I believe wholeheartedly in this statement. I believe we all can draw strength from these wise words as we assist a loved one along their journey back to spirit.

What Your Loved One *May Be* Psychically Experiencing at this Level

During the ninth level, the transition continues, as does the transmutation into the field of omnipresence while the soul multi-tasks, existing on both sides of the veil simultaneously. The living may (or may not) distinctly experience the feeling of their loved one's presence directly following their death around the home, during their funeral, or at any services.

When that supportive presence seems to dissipate or become non-existent (or, if you did not feel it at all) those of us in the physical world can become fear-filled because we believe we have lost connection to our newly passed loved one. The transitioning spirit-body is "busy" attending to the terms and review of the Akashic Record of their completed incarnation. It's important for us to remember that they are always there for us, but the degree of the connection can fluctuate. Patience is key.

Healing Strategies for this Level

- If you are present with your loved one at the last moments of their life, try your best to honor the space within the room following their passing. Sit in quiet reverence if at all possible because the level of spirit is intense and can assist you in finding peace in the transition.
- You may want to write about your experience, journaling about your loved one. Acknowledge what you have been through in the experience from your perspective.
- Do not rush this time. Be patient with your grief, allowing yourself time and space.
- Continue to share stories.
- Continue to be grateful for being allowed to witness the experience.
- If you were not able to be present, you can also feel and know all the same experiences from afar. Remember, our loved ones often make a goodbye visit when they choose to transition, so look for the signs and be grateful.

Ninth Level Case Study

As mentioned in the previous chapter, no case study is included at this level, since my work as an energy healer is done after the seventh level of release.

Ninth Level Summary

- The person is "gone," but Spirit is still in transition.
- Now working in infinite love and light residing in all dimensions.
- All vertical veils of the dimensions now fade.
- The person is in the state of "crossing over" into the white light.

PART III

Rituals and Goodbyes

How to Create a Simple
Farewell Ritual

In Western culture, many have become removed from witnessing the actual dying experience as a normal part of life. In my hospice work, I often find myself not only energetically supporting the patient, but also providing guidance to family and loved ones who may not have a deathbed ritual or practice. In these cases, it can be difficult to know what to do when faced with the dying process and saying a final goodbye to their loved one.

There are many ways to commemorate the death of a loved one, from memorial services to wakes to funerals and more. I regularly suggest performing an end-of-life ritual. No matter the specific religion, tradition, or practice, these rituals offer us a powerful way to open our hearts, minds, and bodies to honor the process of life-force energy moving forward in its final effort of release and return to Source. The idea of ceremony and ritual can be a beautiful way to enhance the experience of saying goodbye to a loved one while they are transitioning through the final stages of dying.

An end of life ritual can be as simple as lighting a candle or saying a prayer. Or, it can be as elaborate as designing a full ceremony with family and friends that is in alignment with the dying person's beliefs as well as the space they are residing in and its rules and regulations. These rituals are only limited by our imagination and creativity and should always aspire to honor and highlight the uniqueness of the individual who is dying.

Each deathbed scenario is unique and will ultimately determine elements of the ritual. Find ways to make the experience memorable and personable, working in love versus fear. Death is inevitable, a given, but the way we experience it is limitless. Using the following outline, as suggested by Rev. Dr. David Laurance Bieniek in his book *At the Time of Death: Symbols & Rituals for Caregivers & Chaplains*,[1] can assist in creating a meaningful experience, but should in no way limit the creativity of the process:

- Identify and Communicate the Purpose of the Ritual
- Create and Set Sacred Space
- Personalize the Experience
- Share and Reflect
- Offer Blessings
- Close the Ritual

Identify and Communicate the Purpose of the Ritual

Each death journey is unique, therefore the purpose of the deathbed ritual or ceremony needs to be determined by the condition of the loved one who is dying. Some rituals are designed to make the dying person more comfortable, offering peace of mind. Other reasons can include creating space for others to gather or saying a final goodbye. It can also offer an opportunity to forgive, release, atone, converse, and share. Ritual performed with a responsive dying person is more participatory, along the lines of healing, whereas when working with a non-responsive person, the effort is designed more as a final goodbye. Comparatively, rituals experienced at the actual point of death and beyond are more about release and mourning.

Every situation also depends on the particular needs of the participants and the location. For example, a private home, a nursing home, or a hospital will all have different rules, regulations, or personal considerations to take into account. Understanding the individual scenario will help clarify the ritual's purpose and design.

---

1 see Rev. Dr. David Laurance Bieniek, *At the Time of Death: Symbols & Rituals for Caregivers & Chaplains* (Berkeley, CA: Apocryphile Press, 2019), 55.

Create and Set Sacred Space

Setting a space for ritual offers a chance for those involved to celebrate the dying person's life and can include those present as well as those who are not able to be in attendance. When it comes to setting the sacred space, again, each case is unique to the situation and its surroundings. It can be as simple as ringing a bell or as orchestrated as full ritual. Oftentimes when a person is in a hospice situation, the family has already begun to set intentional space within and throughout the room by placing pictures as well as sending or bringing personal mementos.

This intentional practice of setting a sacred space can be expanded for any ceremony by including ritual items such as candles, oils, artifacts, albums, photos, special gifts, blankets, artwork, or anything that has special ties to the dying person or the family and friends holding vigil. It is all about creating the dying person's "living memorial space" while they are still present and able to celebrate their life with those they love and cherish. If a family member or friend is not physically able to be at bedside, they can still be included in the ceremony by connecting intentionally, using prayer, or even through technology.

The physical location of the deathbed occurrence may or may not limit the levels of creativity when it comes to setting ritual space with regard to facility rules and regulations or even family and household belief systems. Examine any boundaries or policies on issues like sound levels, music, candle fire or flame, number of people, and more. Also be sensitive to the dying person's state of being in terms of reaction to noise and activity.

Personalize the Experience

Personalizing the ritual or ceremony can be something as effortless as playing music, to a coordinated live ceremony. This again is an area where the dying person's life directly reflects what might be used to engage the senses and honor the loved one, whether that's through sounds, smells, sight, touch, or taste. Incorporate elements to personalize the ritual space by using tools to grow the experience and involve others. Consider using essential oils to not only enhance the smell and feel of the room, but also to anoint and bless their body by directly applying them on your loved one as a sign of honor and respect.

Personal pieces, articles, or items used through any stage of deathbed ceremony become talismans imprinted with the energy of the ritual and are important touchstones for the family and friends left behind. They can be useful and comforting in the grieving process and incorporated into future celebrations of life, evoking feelings of connection, love, and support.

From reading poems and Bible versus, to fresh flowers, family heirlooms, playing musical instruments, hands-on healing, religious artifacts, and more, the opportunities for personalization are only limited by the time and energy put into the ritual. They are an expression of both the person who is journeying and those supporting it—past, present, and even future.

Share and Reflect

Many of us wait to eulogize someone we have lost until after their death, whereas a ritual or ceremony experienced at the deathbed can be a beautiful opportunity to reflect and share memories prior to the person dying. This can offer anyone involved the chance to find acceptance, release, forgiveness, and even joy—all of which can directly assist the dying person's chakra system in its shut-down effort and allow them an easier transition in death.

With regard to sharing and reflecting, it makes no difference if the dying person is identified as responsive or non-responsive, as anything shared is always received either physically, mentally, or telepathically. The energetic beauty of words is felt as much as heard. Those in a non-responsive state are well aware of reflection, intention, and conversation not only from those physically present, but also from anyone sending blessings from afar. This is because the energy moves on a telepathic level of the subconscious as another form of prayer. For this reason, sharing is a vital part of ritual and can be healing for everyone involved.

Offer Blessings

The term "blessings" can mean different things to different people, from religious prayers to poems and song. There is no right or wrong way to do this. The energy here is directed toward the dying person versus the above reflection designed as a sharing of energy among everyone involved. Blessings can be verbal as well as physical, such as the actual use of oils and bathing the body. Those participating in offering a blessing may have family, cultural, or religious views that determine what is appropriate, but remember, the dying person is the one being honored and blessed at this time. Alignment to their personal integrity is key.

Close the Ritual

The effort of any ceremony or ritual ends with a closing element as a way to release the sacred space. There is no need to necessarily physically leave the space or the dying loved one's side to "close" any ritual. Following a ritual, many will choose to stay and immerse themselves in the energy of the celebration. Instead, the closing is an intentional, mental release of the combined ritualistic effort that has taken place. This allows the ceremonial energies to continue to do its job of release. Intentional closing can be as simple as ringing a chime, blowing out a candle, designated words, a handshake, a hug, or a kiss goodbye.

Ritual at the
Point of Death

If you do have the honor of being present at another's actual point of death, be grateful. You are witnessing one of the greatest miracles of life, death and eventual rebirth. Sadly, most of us are feeling such tremendous shock and grief that we often miss the very real miracle playing out before our eyes as someone fully transitions or biologically takes their last human breath.

Identify and Communicate the Purpose of the Ritual

The entire purpose here is just to be present in the sacred moment and allow whatever your humanness needs to do to experience it all, including shock, relief, sadness, and joy—the rollercoaster of emotion and awareness.

Create and Set Sacred Space

You are within the most sacred of spaces at this time. Do not rush anything as you do your best to not *DO*, but rather, just *BE* in the moment. There are many benevolent beings hard at work within the room. You can review the stages of death earlier in the book to remind yourself of all that is in the works that we cannot visually see, but certainly can feel. Immerse yourself into the energy of this sacred time and space and be mindful of others without expectation. Sitting with a loved one who is taking their final breath or who has just died does not have to be a scary time, but for some it may well be, so do not judge your actions or that of another in vigil. Just allow. Everyone has different reactions to death and loss, and some need to find separate space to feel safe. Take cues from others in the room as to their needs. Trust your instincts.

Personalize the Experience

The elements here begin to shift from ritual to more tactical with the eventual need to make some end-of-life decisions if they have not already been made in terms of what to do next. Take your time.

Share and Reflect

For many, this is again a very pertinent time to share stories and this can be very healing for those left behind. There may be those in attendance that choose to kiss the body, hug the body, or even cuddle with it. There is no right or wrong on how to move through these phases. Be kind to others and honor their personal passage through shock, grief, or relief. Do your best to not judge.

Offer Blessings and Close the Ritual

The final, final goodbye for the body is difficult for many, even if there is also a sense of relief that our loved one is no longer struggling or suffering. The grim realization that our loved one is really gone can be daunting, and however one chooses to say a final blessing or farewell is unique and personal. Patience for yourself and others is first and foremost. In this phase, it may also be important to include those family or friends who cannot be present in person. There are many ways with technology to include them if you/they choose.

What I *Psychically See* During Deathbed Ritual

We often hear stories from people who feel as if a deceased loved one energetically attends his or her memorial service or funeral. These amazing stories include accounts of spirit activity, bizarre synchronicities, or miraculous events happening during the ritual itself and the surrounding hours and days. So, is this even possible?

In my personal opinion as a lightworker, the answer is yes. It is normal for a deceased person to attend their own service or funeral after they have died and returned to Source. Oftentimes during a deathbed ritual, funeral, or memorial service, I *psychically see* the energy of the dying or deceased person in attendance and find it fascinating how much our loved ones are still around us.

I experience this with what is psychically known as "inner-vision" using the third eye, as well as "outer-vision" of my actual physical eyes. Inner vision sight sees the image in the mind's eye—like a movie, idea, or scene played out as a knowing sensation. In this capacity, I have seen the deceased amongst their family hovering alongside them or floating over them, not as a full apparition or spirit, but more along the lines of energy and color, which is often white, pink, and green—representative of love energy.

What is amazing about these times is that family and friends often physically sense the person who has died through smell, touch, or other senses. Even those who have never sensed energy from the beyond before can have very clear and real experiences of their loved one who has passed.

During ritual ceremonies, I have physically seen with outer-vision clear, well-defined energy signatures pulsating above the bed, casket, or memorial urn. These are more like a kaleidoscope of geometric shapes and color. My clairaudient and cognitive skills of psychically hearing and knowing has engaged in conversation with the dying or deceased during their ceremonies and sometimes has included a message for someone in attendance.

I also frequently experience the sentient or "feeling-sensations" of a dying or deceased person at their rituals and celebrations. This can include a pocket of space within the room or surrounding a person that moves the energy at a different temperature, either hot or cold, and may or may not include an emotion. Additionally, the cemetery burial ritual is another place I often find the spirit of the deceased person making their presence known in unique calling-card ways, often incorporating nature's elements of wind in huge gusts for example, or symbolic birds that distinctly chatter a final farewell, or the appearance of a single dragonfly that hovers above. They are always around us, it is up to us to be *present* enough to receive the PRESENT or gift of their continued connection.

While following the process in this book, you now realize that a fully crossed person transmutes back to Source energy which then allows them the opportunity to become what is known as omnipresent and able to traverse all dimensions of light and planes of reality. Therefore, they are able to attend any service or visit any loved one in any location as they choose.

Additionally, a recent death of the physical body still has the auric body in transition. This can take days to complete, again, allowing them the energetic opportunity to attend their own service simply to celebrate their life and the life of those they love. This is very common and makes complete sense to me as an energy worker. The auric field will continue to transmute and transition over the following days, and this is why sometimes we feel their presence and then don't. It is not something to fear as they are continually in transition and will always be available to us in heart-space.

Whatever you decide to do during this end-of-life process, remember—the ultimate goal of the deathbed ritual is *PEACE*: *peace for the heart, peace of mind, peace for the body, peace for energetic transition through death, peace for family and friends and those in attendance and those sending blessing from afar, and peace for the journey as a whole.*

The Grieving Process and Helpful Strategies for Moving through It

Grief

Grief is a natural reaction to loss and is something each of us will go through at some point in our lives, whether it is due to the loss of a loved one, a job, or even a belief. When something we love is taken away, grief is our natural, suffering-based response, which can affect not only our emotions, but also our physical and mental health.

When we lose a loved one, we experience grief based upon our personal beliefs about loss, death, or what grief should look like. We've learned a lot of these beliefs from our family, our upbringing, and our society without giving them too much thought. Most people's foundational beliefs teach them to fear death, hence we also fear its counterpart, which is grief. Experiences of bereavement, mourning, pain, sorrow, and heartache are often very fear-filled, yet these are natural steps in the journey of death and grief.

I have been a certified hospice worker for many years, supporting the end-of-life journey for both the patients and the families involved. Our human meat-and-bone-body lives through the use of our energetic-spiritual-auric bodies. When we die, our body seeks to release these auric bodies to help us disconnect from the physical, three-dimensional world. As a hospice worker, my job is to energetically assist the dying person by helping them release these auric bodies from the three-dimensional world (physical, emotional, and mental fields) so the dying person can return to the *spiritual* field with ease and grace.

Energy work during and after death assists the transition process for not only the person, but their loved ones holding vigil. When I'm able to offer a psychic spiritual vision of the death process, it allows family members and friends to see the three-dimensional world a bit differently, and presents a new set of tools for navigating the grief process that normally follows the death of a loved one.

As an energy practitioner, I often work with clients experiencing grief, whether it is due to the loss of a job, moving onward in their lives after a separation or divorce, falling out of favor with family or friends, or the actual loss of a loved one, either human or pet. Regardless of the kind of loss my clients are experiencing, many of their reactions to the passing are similar.

Typical Reactions to Grief

Many clients experience tears during grief, but some do not. Crying is a normal and natural response for the body, which helps us move the energies through and release the emotions. Some people, however, find themselves not able to cry and this can be due to many reasons, such as how they were brought up or feeling as if they should retain a sense of control.

When people do not cry during a time of loss, they often feel as if they are broken somehow. Pressuring yourself or someone else to cry during the grieving period can be harmful to the ongoing experience. Some even find the opposite emotion, laughter, is their form of release. The off-handed or sometimes inappropriate giggles or smirks can help the body perform the same emotional release as someone else who is shedding tears.

Other reactions to loss can include, but are not limited to, trembling or shaking, pounding heart, stuck throat, upset stomach, racing thoughts, shock, disbelief, guilt, anger, sorrow, depression, and disconnection. How we grieve is a personal experience and there is no one way, nor right way, to do it. It is a process, and there is no time-clock as to how one moves through each stage. Some people move through the process in weeks or months, others in years. Some choose to never move forward.

Hospice organizations frequently use the teachings of Elisabeth Kubler-Ross and David Kessler to clarify these "stages" of grieving a death. In their opinion, there are five stages to a typical grief process: denial, anger, bargaining, depression, and acceptance. Ross and Kessler present these stages as tools to help the survivors recognize and support what they may be feeling or experiencing following a death or deep personal loss. It's important to note that not everyone goes through all stages in a prescribed order. In fact, I find in my work that most people jump throughout the stages, repeating some, while skipping others.

What are the Five Stages of Grief?

Denial

Denial is the first stage of grief because this is the shocking, numbing realization that your world is forever changed. It may feel like everything is crashing down around you or you may refuse to acknowledge it and deny it is even happening. As a human being, you are experiencing this reaction mostly in your mental body and auric field. You are trying to make sense of things, based on your mind-programming, which is running at a rapid pace and almost blocking off the emotional field. This "blocking" of the emotional field creates the numbing effect throughout the physical body.

This stage is important for the energy bodies because it allows them to begin to connect and support one another. So give yourself time and patience to move through this Stage of Denial at the pace that is unique to you. The more patience you have, the more the emotional field will be able to begin to surface when it feels safe to do so. The numb feeling also protects the physical body to get ready to traverse the next stage of grief, which is usually anger.

Anger

Anger is a very necessary stage in the process of mourning, but it is critical to move into, and then through, this stage. If you hold on to the energy of anger, it will eventually cause dis-ease or disease your own body and manifest as physical, emotional, or mental symptoms.

My suggestion is to *move into your anger* by examining it rather than stuffing it. If you do choose to stuff it, it *will still be there* creating the foundation for potential dis-ease to come. Befriend your own body during this Stage of Anger, and remember that anger is only the surface emotion to the *energy of fear.* So examine what it is that you are afraid of regarding the recent loss. There are usually many underlying layers to this stage, and it is the anchored fear-based beliefs that you want to unearth, examine, and make peace with.

This stage also can ignite challenging thoughts like, *"Why did God let this happen?"* or *"Why didn't I stop him/her."* This is when you may want to revisit how to honor the concept of the *Soul Contract* and *Akashic Records* explained earlier in this book. Honoring another's Soul Contract allows your heart to open and heal by acknowledging that person gets to die and move forward on their soul path because they chose to from a Higher place.

Bargaining

This is the stage I usually see people experiencing when they get a fatal diagnosis for themselves or their loved one. It is also experienced when family or friends are supporting the final stages of the death process and holding vigil for the impending passing. At either point, most people will be willing to do just about anything to change the path in process, including bargaining on behalf of themselves for the one dying. Many will strike a bargain with "God" to change the outcome *"If you do this, then I will do that."*

During this stage it is also critical to examine the acceptance of the Akashic Record of the person moving forward in their death journey. When we put conditions on our love for someone by bargaining for a different outcome than what their Record currently is dictating as their journey, it is as if we are saying that we will love them more if they will change their outcome or change the path of their journey to fit what is comfortable for me, the one who remains.

Other bargaining statements include the "if only's" that harbor the feelings of guilt for not being in the right place at the right time, missing the opportunity to again change the outcome. Guilt will move the energies back into the mental field and begin to run old tapes of victim programming, including messages of: *"I was not there, it is somehow my fault, I am not good enough, I was not able to change the outcome,"* and this will then lead to the next Stage of Depression.

Depression

Depression can take many forms as the grief is settling into the body and the life of the person left without their loved one. Depression is an appropriate and normal part to the mourning process and should not always automatically be seen as slipping into a mentally unstable state or becoming ill.

The deep sadness of loss and how it affects your present life can be overwhelming and lonely and can affect your behavior. Withdrawing from life for a period of adjustment is common and is helpful to the energy bodies, which are working to arrive at some sort of resolution, balance, and state of healing.

At this stage, it is important to examine the actual layers of the depressed state. Take time and patience to unravel the physical, emotional, and mental situations causing depression as well as the underlying feelings, which can move you to the next Stage of Accepting that you will now be living without that person.

Acceptance

This stage can be a bit confusing because some feel like this word "acceptance" means *"getting over it"* or *"being all done grieving now"* and that is simply not the case. Most people don't ever really *get over* a death. We move through it and onward from it.

Instead, this stage is all about accepting the situation and the reality of it. I believe this stage is where one can really learn to trust in one's Higher Self and spiritual connection to Source. It is an opportunity to connect with our loved one working with a different set of tools and learning to work with and honor their energy body, instead of mourning the loss of the meat-and-bone one.

To move into this stage, find ways to connect with the new version of their Higher vibrational Self. When you actively seek to connect in healthy ways, you can find the joy and wonder of the signs they send via magical calling cards such as birds, special songs, or a whiff of a personal fragrance. This stage is where we regain our birthright to use our psychic senses and stretch our skills beyond the three-dimensional world into the magic of the beyond.

Coping

Most of us fear death itself, but coping with the loss of a loved one is probably one of life's hardest challenges. Experiencing the pain of grief and mourning death is an important piece of shifting one's energy to clear the cell trauma of the loss. Many people's family or societal beliefs give them the message to run from or stuff away the emotions of grief.

Many adults try to cover up their grief to protect the feelings of others, especially if there are children involved. Others have grown up with the messages of anger when it comes to the grief process and run the victim "Why Me?" programming, which keeps them from moving onward with life following the loss of a loved one. We are raised with many mixed messages on how to cope with death, and will ultimately face and deal with grief differently.

Grief is as unique as the individual. Not everyone grieves the same, and there is certainly no appropriate time-clock attached to the process. My goal as an energy practitioner and instructor is to offer knowledge of the soul and its Akashic Record. Prior to a human incarnation, each soul drafts their unique Akashic Record, or Book of Life, which contains the elements of not only their life, but also their death. When we acknowledge the concept that everyone "gets to die," this can soften and sometimes even eliminate the *Stage of Anger* to help us move more swiftly into the *Stage of Acceptance*.

Finding acceptance of the person's soul decision, in the way they die, the time they die, and with whom they die at their side, offers those left behind a tool to assist them in moving through these stages of grief.

In my work with clients traversing through these stages of death and looking for healing, I see many stuck in the emotional and mental trappings of guilt, victimization, confusion, and despair. This includes the *"if only's"* and the *"what if's"* that so many struggle with. During healing sessions, I will cut the energetic cords between the living and the deceased, cords that still fuel these stages, to release the life-force drain that affects the living person left grieving. Some of the reasons these cords exist are the guilt-ridden concepts of: *not getting there in time, not being able to communicate certain words or atonements before their loved one passes, or "why and how did this happen to me?"*

I counsel the client that the soul chooses its death, and from a higher plane of existence, it fully knows what it is doing. So we can assist this by cutting these cords, which allows us to move forward. Honoring the soul contract allows us to move forward and experience these stages of grief with a better understanding and acceptance, while still acknowledging the reality of the loss and finding that spiritual balance. It does not mean that you are okay with the loss, much less like it. We are still human, after all, and energetically it is important to grieve.

Some Tips on How to Deal with Grief

- Do it *YOUR* way. Everyone moves through the process of grieving and mourning differently, so own your unique version and be sure to take care of yourself first.
- Seek outside support when needed, and seek inner solace when needed.
- Do not hide from your true emotions, including the pain of loss.
- Be aware that a new loss can indeed trigger an old one. With this can come unexpected feelings and emotions.
- Stay physically, emotionally, and mentally grounded by making time for yourself and be sure that some of this time is *QUIET* time.
- Practice relaxation techniques that keep you connected to your body and to Mother Earth. Your Root Chakra is the life-force point that holds the "feeling safe" energies. Make sure to honor your feelings of safety as you move through life now, without

that person you have recently lost. Examine what your new version of safe looks like, feels like, sounds like, and adjust accordingly.

- Schedule time to cultivate joy in your life, include friendships that support your path, find a new interest, and have some fun without guilt attached.
- Relax with a good book, a hot bath filled with glorious essences like lavender oil, or enjoy a great glass of wine by a blazing fire.
- Take care of your meat-and-bone-body by getting plenty of rest, good nourishing foods, and water.
- Do your best to reestablish your routine or create a new one. After the loss of one who has been integral in our routine life, it is important to find a new rhythm, a new flow, that offers freedom and passion or comfort and familiarity.
- When you have a good day, do not allow any guilt of moving onward to overshadow your joy in any way.
- And last, have patience. There is no end to how we handle life or death, there is only the journey.

Experiencing the death of a loved one can be life-altering. The ones left behind oftentimes need to modify their daily routine, and sometimes, their entire lifestyle, especially if their level of grief moves into long-term depression, feelings of isolation, and abandonment. This is a time to reach out for assistance. Allow yourself to fully grieve in your own way, in your own timeline. Keep talking and sharing with those that love you, and take one day at a time. Make sure you have a support system or call a professional to assist in the process.

Epilogue

When we have created (or remembered) our new understanding of all of this, we will realize that death does not, technically, energetically exist.

We will know that our opportunity to learn and to grow is never over, and that the time to be rewarded or punished for how we lived our lives will never come, because life is not a reward and punishment proposition. Rather, it is a process of continuous and unending growth, expansion, self-expression, self-creation, and self-fulfillment.

One of the reasons I wrote this book is to help others *see* death by use of energetic psychic eyes. Death can indeed be understood to be simply and only a transition—a glorious shifting in the experience of the soul, a change in our level of consciousness, a freedom-giving, pain-releasing, awareness-expanding transmutation of the eternal process of evolution.

I have been privileged to be a part of many amazing death journeys, and for that, I am forever grateful. We humans can find a different way to experience death. We can understand that death does not have to be something to be feared. Death can be seen as an eternal part of the wonderful experience called Life itself.

I wanted this book to help others talk about and experience death with freedom. Replacing undue sadness by expanding old thought forms. Finding new insights and knowledge of how the soul works, insights that can come from honoring the soul contract, the Akashic Record, and the entire reason for being a human BEing.

I wanted people to find a different way to not feel compelled to cling to life when they are suffering and dying, because they'll truly know that there is nothing *but* life.

I wanted people to know that we are never alone in life or in death.

I was asked once in a radio interview what my final words were as the show was coming to an end and I said this: *"Live as if you are dying because you will energetically die how you were living. Clear and balance your chakra system in terms of releasing fears NOW while you are still alive on this Earth. It will make your death process easier, but it will also make your human journey a heck of a lot more fun!!"*

Namaste!

Appendices

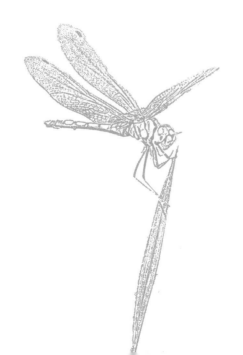

Appendix I

Other Death Experiences

Some Additional Death Experiences
We May Encounter in Life

Miscarriage

I am the mother of four children, with my oldest in his 30s at the writing of this book. It sometimes feels like only yesterday when I suffered a miscarriage between my first and second child. It took me close to four years to conceive again, mostly because of the fear I held within my physical body as well as the emotional and mental bodies. No matter how much my family and friends tried to support me, it was terrifying and confusing and an extremely personal journey.

When I work with clients in my healing practice who have also suffered a miscarriage, I tell them the same thing I chose to tell myself—that the soul of the incoming child chose to not come fully into the existence of the human experience at this particular time. That this decision was made from a higher place than our 3-D world, and there was nothing I was supposed to do or not do to change this soul's decision. No fear, and certainly no guilt I held, would be able to change that.

During this difficult time, I tried my best to embrace the concept of the soul contract. I tried to understand, from a place of Source, that I had also contracted to undergo this experience for a reason. That reason may not be clear in the moment of grief, certainly, but I believe there *is* a reason. We have no way of knowing how an incoming soul chooses whether or not to fully arrive. Perhaps the universal timeline needs to be in direct alignment with the Book of Life it was creating. It may not be the right sex, birth order, vibration on the Earth plane of existence, and so on. There is no way for us to know, and we can only speculate. My personal opinion is that we do not *have to* know, even if our human ego desperately *wants to* know.

We sometimes can move through our grief and suffering easier by honoring the soul's decision to not come in fully at this time. We can trust that incoming souls know exactly what they are doing for their purposes and learn to respect that.

We also have to acknowledge that the loss of a child in utero is much the same as any other loss. If it is our own experience, we need to give ourselves the time and space to mourn. If we find ourselves supporting a friend or family member who has suffered a miscarriage, the same holds true.

Sometimes my clients experience the feeling that a soul personality will always be there for them on this side of the veil as well as the other side. When doing client sessions, I frequently find the soul essence of the miscarriage will join us in my healing space to assist. I sometimes even receive messages when the miscarried soul decided to change the vehicle for their human experience and instead incarnate as another human form within the same immediate or surrounding family, manifesting perhaps as a sibling or a relative. This is why we often find a parent or relative feels as if they already know a child when they first arrive into the family. It is important to not make judgment on anyone who has a feeling that their miscarried child has indeed returned in *another body,* because oftentimes, this is true.

Understanding the soul contract, the Akashic Record, and the free will of Source in no way removes the grief and pain caused during this difficult time. But opening our heads and our hearts to the soul contract knowledge can, over time, help us consider the bigger picture at work, and that from a higher place we are part of that plan, and we will see our loved one again when we decide the time is right.

Suicide

In my work as a healer, I have encountered many scenarios of suicide. There is no way to make a blanket statement about suicide because every story is unique, and the spiritual elements involved are specific to every individual case. I have worked with crossed soul essences who have committed suicide and hold degrees of regret for their actions, and are working to atone, but this is not always true. Sometimes these spirits fully accept their decision.

In my practice of clearing and crossing, I have also worked with many spirits who have not fully gone to the light due to the fear attached to the act of suicide. These spirits are stuck in our human beliefs of Hell and its consequences. To understand what happens when a spirit gets stuck, it's first important to recognize free will is a gift. As a human expression of Source, we are gifted and endowed free will and free choice. When we choose to end our human experience with a suicide, we endure the consequences in all planes of existence. This means when I use suicide to escape my current troubles in this life, I still have work to do in terms of energy and spirit that I cannot escape. That work is to atone, find peace, and overcome the fears we endure in this lifetime. Our work is to find compassion and forgiveness, and then, return fully to love. When people are operating from confusion and desperation, it's hard to understand that as a soul, *we still need to do the work whether we are on this side of the veil or not.* Therefore, in my opinion, it is often best to do your work on this side of the veil, in your human experience, where you can embrace growth and clear karmic debt associated with the life that you're struggling with all while you are here in your physical form.

Soul contracts can be an integral component of most suicides. We contract with one another prior to our incarnation as a human expression of Source. These people we've contracted with at a soul-level hold spiritual importance for us in our human experience. I call this group of people our "soul-pod." Soul-pods include our loved ones from many lifetimes—good, bad, and ugly—collectively working out our karmic debt. Suicide overrides certain scenarios that are part of our contract with our soul-pod—this is often why suicide is such a complex loss. Our friends, family, and even enemies are all contracted to work collectively here with us, and oftentimes a suicide will interfere with the initial contractual agreements. Sometimes, however, the suicide may be an actual part of the initial soul contract to learn lessons and balance past karmic debt. The soul contract, and people involved in them as the families, friends, and enemies affected, always offer opportunities for spiritual growth. The partner, mother, father, child, sibling, or friend that is affected by the suicide act, may indeed have actually contracted with the person performing the suicide to learn something in their own soul path experience. When this is the case, I believe these spirits cross over the veil with more ease and have the potential to learn their lessons quicker and heal faster than those who may have significantly altered their soul contract. Again, this is a very blanket statement and may not resonate as totally true in terms of each individual case.

Through my work as a healer, I have assisted many spirits who have committed suicide and not fully crossed to the light because of a belief system held here in fear of what they may encounter in terms of God, heaven or hell. It is important to evaluate and examine our belief systems because they ultimately assist us in transitioning and crossing fully into the light. There is a lot of programmed fear attached to suicide, and the belief that we are prohibited to fully cross most often comes from religious dogma and societal upbringing.

I personally don't believe in what we call or perceive as hell, at least, not the one our religious dogma has painted as a horrific place of fire and eternal damnation, nor do I believe that those who commit suicide "go there." I have confidence that you are never alone and are indeed greeted by your loved ones, your guides and angels, and that these benevolent beings are there to assist, nurture, and teach throughout your entire journey. Free will of suicide offers us the ability to make bad decisions when we are lost in our desolation and sadness—when we have lost self-love. But we are all born from love, we are made from love, and we have the ability to return to love.

I have also worked with clients who are so desolate from the death of a loved one that they feel taking their own life offers them the chance to reunite. Again, it does not work this way in terms of energy. When you are in a fearful state and commit suicide, the fear-based vibration your soul is holding will cross at a lower resonation. This denser energy will not align with your loved one who has already passed and crossed, as they retain a much higher vibration of omnipresence. Lower vibration carries conditional fear—higher vibration carries unconditional love. This does not mean that you will never see or encounter your loved ones, but it does mean the souls will not continually *hang out together,* so to speak. It is important to honor the fact that your free will choice to commit suicide does indeed have consequences.

We have no right to judge or assume anything when it comes to the act of suicide. It is not for anyone to condemn the person who committed the act, or the actions or feelings of those involved in the outer circle. We often take ownership of other people's choices, and we actually have no right to own them. Families often carry stigma associated with suicide. For me, this is not honoring the soul contract or free will decision, and it is taking the energy of the act into your own field and making it about *you* rather than honoring another's choice. Often it is the survivors who need assistance in dealing with survivor's guilt because they feel they should have known, changed, or prevented the suicide from happening. Every spirit I have talked to from the other side of the veil has reiterated that there was no way anyone could have prevented it or changed it.

Suicide challenges us all, but it can invite us to ask and seek deeper questions, to find bigger and better ways to look at spirit. It gives us an opportunity to see how it is that we actually view life from our own truths and how we connect to those truths for ourselves and for others.

Loss of a Companion Animal

Being a mother of four children, I have presided over numerous animal funeral services and rituals. Our backyard is home to an extensive pet cemetery filled with everything from our family bunny who decided to die on Easter morning to Guinea pigs, dogs, fish, bearded dragons, and more. We had a Wheaton Terrier who lived for fourteen years, and many of those years included me doing healing work to reignite her field and keep her moving for a couple more months at a time until finally it was time to let her go. As a family, we have had the difficult task of putting down several of our pets due to old age or illness.

Almost every one of us has encountered some type of pet loss, and each of us handles this scenario in our own unique way. Pets become a part of our family, and losing them can be traumatic. Being faced with a choice of euthanasia is even more difficult as there can be so much guilt attached to this decision. Some of my clients struggle with *if they did the right thing in putting their animal to sleep,* while some even feel they have committed a version of murder in deciding upon and following through with euthanasia. I, too, struggled with this decision with three of our beloved four-legged friends that faced terminal illness or simply lost the quality of their life due to advanced age. It is never an easy choice.

Oftentimes our animals choose to re-enter our lives in another animal form years later, and sometimes we can even feel that we *know them.* Our deceased animals can also assist us from across the veil in many ways. When our Wheaton Terrier named Harriet died, she came to me in a meditation to clearly tell us which dog to choose as the next family dog from a long list of names we were pondering from animal rescue. She told us that *"Dudley was the one"* and when we went to look up Dudley, it was the last dog we would have picked due to the scraggly photo posted on the rescue site. But in honoring Harriet's message, we indeed bought Dudley and he turned out to be one of the best dogs our family has ever had the privilege to own. A true soul guide in dog form was offered to us, all thanks to the guidance of our beloved deceased Harriet.

Grieving a pet is a process much like any loved one, with vulnerable emotions and feelings that need to be honored and shared. Similar to the human experience, we need to respect the soul contract they have chosen and take one day at a time to heal. Usually, we will find our grief will subside with time and patience.

Appendix II

Transition Stages and Healing Strategies at a Glance

First Level of Transition

1st Dimension of Light / Root Chakra / Auric Etheric Body
Shuts down the consciousness of *"all we experience"* as the *BODY* of Mother Earth Energies and Planet Consciousness

First Level Summary

- It is a fearful period for many and can be confusing.
- Loss of material items may create a sense of panic.
- This a time to be fully present for the dying person.
- Share unconditional love to assist family, friend, or medical attendant by working physically, emotionally, mentally, and spiritually.
- Assist your loved one with verbal or telepathic conversation or prayer.
- This is the beginning stage of the death process in energy and usually takes a number of hours to transition.

What I *Psychically See* at this Level

During this time, I psychically *see* an energetic release within the human body in terms of the person's programmed belief systems. This happens in the lower trunk of the body—the hips, the legs, the "meat and bone" of the body. The colors of the energy throughout the room that the person is in usually feels to me somewhat dense and oftentimes fear-based. This can be a heavy feeling. A thick feeling. The more fear the person carries in their field, the thicker the energy of the room. The actual auric colors of the energy within the room are somewhat like muddy or charcoal blobs that move in slow patterns.

As I work to assist the dying person through this phase, their root or base chakra will eventually slow to the point of stopping and then it will go dark. My job is to assist them in releasing any fears with regards to *stuff* and material things—knowing that their possessions are no longer important. I also work to help them know they are safe. That all is OK with allowing their body to progress through this journey. Telepathically talking them through this concept helps to release any energy blocks.

As they continue to release any blocks holding these programmed patterns of beliefs, eventually their first dimension of light will dissolve as does their etheric body of the aura. It is a transmuting of energy—a returning to Source.

What Your Loved One *May Be* Psychically Experiencing at this Level

Because this chakra release usually happens at the beginning levels of transition, the dying person is typically experiencing more 3-D encounters with their own programmed beliefs rather than interaction with spirit-helpers (who will arrive to assist in later stages).

Confronting personal beliefs can give rise to mental and emotional fears that play out much like a reel of memories, similar to an old-time movie speeding through the person's consciousness container. If the person encountered fear-based people, places, and situations throughout their life, this movie reel offers the ability to examine, forgive, and release these experiences. Most of the psychic connections the dying person brings forth at this level have to do with revisiting their sense of safety, BEing, and self-worth.

Healing Strategies for this Level

- Allow yourself to be as present as much as you choose for your loved one, either in person or from afar, *only when balanced with making sure you take care of yourself* in terms of nourishment, sleep, and support.
- If there is any unfinished business with the person, try your best to resolve these issues, if possible. If that is not possible,

try to write down your unresolved business, and release any negative holds via prayer, a burning ceremony, or whatever you choose to do to allow the issues to move onward.

- As the caregiver, allow yourself to go through all the emotions, feelings, and stages of grieving.
- Do your best through conversation to reassure your loved one that all of their things will be taken care of—their home, their belongings, their treasures—offering them solace that they can let go of *stuff*.
- Express your thoughts and feelings with your loved one, either out loud or in your heart.

Second Level of Transition

2nd Dimension of Light / Sacral Chakra / Auric Emotional Body

Final Release of *"all we create"* as the *MIND* of Mother Earth Energies and Planet Consciousness

Second Level Summary

- There is an emotional release of Earth-bound relationships.
- Emotional blocks for the person can include unresolved issues with family, friends, and loved ones.
- They may be harboring fear of encountering a deceased relative or friend.
- They may have fear of God, heaven, or hell.
- There is an ego-related release, causing a pull-effect to the energies within the room.
- It is key to assist the dying person with unconditional sharing of divine love.

What I *Psychically See* at this Level

During this time, I psychically *see* an energetic release within the human body in the belly area. The actual auric colors of the energy within the room are still somewhat like muddy blobs that move in slow patterns, but as we move through this phase, the patterns will begin to take on a bit of a lighter flow. Also, the fields of energy

AN ENERGY HEALER'S BOOK OF DYING

will begin to bring in a bit of color into the blobs of energy moving throughout the room.

As I work to assist the dying person through this phase, their sacral chakra will eventually slow to the point of stopping and then it will go dark. My job is to assist them in releasing any concerns with relationships, emotions, and fears. This can be a difficult time for many to let go of their loved ones, so I also work to help them know they are safe, as are any loved ones that they may be leaving behind. Telepathically talking them through this concept helps to release any energy blocks. As they continue to release, their second dimension of light will dissolve as does their emotional body of the aura. It is a transmuting of energy—a returning to Source.

What Your Loved One *May Be* Psychically Experiencing at this level

During this stage, your loved one continues to release 3-D beliefs and programming, but now the focus is on his or her relationships with others. I find many dying people take this time to psychically visit those who may not be in attendance with them or holding vigil for their death. The psychic self energetically is omnipresent, meaning the consciousness can astrally travel anywhere within any time-space continuum to make amends or find forgiveness for self or others.

These experiences can range from the person psychically visiting a loved one who has already passed to connecting with someone who is still in physical human form on Earth. Reasons for a psychic visit may be to atone for the past, make a love-connection, or send a message.

For some, this can be a time when they begin to better understand the process of how soul transition works in omnipresent love, meaning that whether deceased or still in the process of dying, our energy has the ability to connect with loved ones at any time and in any place. For others, the realization of omnipresent love comes much later in their transition during the heart chakra release in the fourth and fifth levels.

Healing Strategies for this Level
- Make sure you and all caregivers are getting sufficient rest, food, and fresh air.
- Talk to other family members about their feelings on the journey of your loved one and share your true feelings with them.
- Review your relationship with your loved one and see if there is anything unfinished that needs attention.
- Forgive anything that is holding any unease in any way.
- Thank your loved one for their relationship with you.
- Reassure the person that all others involved will be looked after and taken care of, allowing them to move onward with no worries.
- Express your thoughts and feelings with your loved one, either out loud or in your heart.

Third Level of Transition

3rd Dimension of Light / Solar Plexus Chakra / Auric Mental Body

Shuts down the consciousness of "*all we experience*" as the *BODY* of Human Form Energies

Third Level Summary

- This is the beginning of letting go of all physical realities of time and physical laws.
- The dying person may physically appear to be struggling. This is the templates releasing—from an energy standpoint, it is a calm release.
- Breathing patterns may become jerky, gurgling, and unsettling to witness.
- The dying person encounters their contrasting dual power sources—the *ME* of human EGO and the *WE* of collective spirit.
- Begins mottling: feet, hands, and sometimes arms begin to turn blackish-blue and blotchy because robust energy centers or chakras are closing.

- Body has web-effect: discoloration of white-ish splotches because very light yellowish lines of auric mental energy body grid are dissolving.
- The energy in the room may be somewhat heavy.

What I *Psychically See* at this Level

During this time, I psychically *see* an energetic release within the human body in terms of the person's programmed ego.

In my opinion, this is one of the most difficult phases for those in attendance, when ironically it is one of the most beautiful phases for the dying person. Because it is such a human release of all physical templates, the physical body seems to be struggling, however the spirit is peacefully surrendering.

Psychically, this is a stage of a beautiful transition in energy. It is a calm and gentle return to the spiritual planes of existence, yet the body can seem to be doing everything but surrendering into the calm. If you are in attendance at this time and are experiencing what you see as struggle, please note that this is similar to a snake shedding an old outgrown skin, wriggling into the freedom of a different body of existence.

The actual auric colors of the energy within the room can seem to fight during this stage as well because this is such a release of ego and physicality. Depending on the person, this energetic imbalance can be slight or significant.

As I work to assist the person through this phase, their solar plexus chakra will eventually slow to the point of stopping and then it will go dark. My job is to assist them in releasing any ego and physical fears. Telepathically talking them through this concept helps to release any energy blocks.

As they continue to release, their third dimension of light will dissolve as does their mental body of the aura. It is a transmuting of energy—a returning to Source.

What Your Loved One *May Be* Psychically Experiencing at this Level

The third level of transition can appear to be one of the most difficult times in the death process for the loved one's physical body, as many seem to struggle physically with jerking movements and rapid breath. That said, their physical self is experiencing another side to this process.

The physical body of consciousness is beginning to fully release, which allows the dying person to remember his or her spiritual body. To the outside world this looks like a struggle, but psychically, it is an introduction of an old beloved friend: their true self. During this time, the body is being flooded with love and light, and you can see this as the web-effects in the auric fields I described earlier.

For most, this is also a welcome relief of *remembering*, remembering what we know in terms of *there is more*. However, for anyone who is fear-filled in ego, power, dominance, and control, this can be a difficult remembering which may extend this chakra release time. Those holding vigil may offer understanding and support via loving thoughts and patience.

Healing Strategies for this Level

- Make sure you and all caregivers are getting sufficient rest, food, and fresh air.
- This is a time for patience for the process. It can be a scary time for some experiences and it is important to remember that some of the physical changes are due to the auric template changes, and if one can honor that transitional experience instead of fear it, that helps the dying person.
- Ask questions of the professionals if this gives you a better sense of knowledge and comfort in this process.
- Acknowledge any of your own fears and anger away from the person's bedside; share your emotions and feelings with others available to you.
- Help others in the room share their feelings and emotions and be tolerant of their grieving processes.

- Begin a journal of your visits and leave a shared book in the room.
- Express your thoughts and feelings with your loved one, either out loud or in your heart.

Fourth Level of Transition

4th Dimension of Light / Heart Chakra or Bridge / Auric Astral Body
Final Release of *"all we create"* as the *MIND* of Human Form Energies

Fourth Level Summary

- Releases all thoughts and ideas that have worked to formulate and manifest the human body.
- Bridges the physical plane to the spiritual plane.
- Can be a very confusing time for those holding vigil for the dying person.
- Seems to be almost a revitalization of the body.
- A flurry of activity or burst of energy, can be puzzling.
- There may be a charged feeling within the room.
- Confusing signals can be misinterpreted by those in attendance.
- Hours of actual death are often fairly short.

What I *Psychically See* at this Level

During this time, I psychically *see* beautiful blobs and swirls of color begin to hover over, above, and around the person. The auric colors are soft swirling orbs of energy floating musically above the person and throughout the room.

Psychically, I also begin to see vertical lines or images floating above the body. This takes the place of any chakra vortexes that I previously saw within the body.

As I work to assist the person through this phase, their heart chakra, now seen as a vertical line, will go dark and then dissolve. My job is to continue to assist them in releasing any fears. Telepathically talking them through this concept helps to release any energy blocks in the human body. I also help them bring in any spiritual assistance they choose to ask for in terms of helpers, guides, and loved ones from spirit.

As they continue to release, their fourth dimension of light will dissolve as does their bridge or astral body of the aura. It is a transmuting of energy—a returning to Source.

What Your Loved One *May Be* Psychically Experiencing at this Level

The floodgates have been opened, and the energy now ramps up as the person becomes aware of the love and light supporting their energetic transition from this point forward. By now most people are beginning to notice their spirit-helpers, usually starting with their guardian angel. Many dying people feel their guardian is stationed at the top of the bedside, over their shoulder.

Additionally, at this phase, the dying person can also become aware of deceased loved ones entering the scene to support the journey, from spouses to parents, grandparents, and even pets. Psychically, many show themselves as simply energy signatures, much like wiggly lines of heat visible above pavement on a scorching day. Others may see a full apparition of how their loved one appeared physically during their life. It all depends on the dying person's beliefs and how they choose to bring in the information.

Healing Strategies for this Level

- Make sure you and all caregivers are getting sufficient rest, food, and fresh air.
- You may want to discuss the wants and needs of a service for your loved one. Choose a favorite poem, prayer, or picture. Determine if this conversation is better discussed in the presence of the dying person or in private with other family members.
- Share great stories and memories at bedside with your loved one, fully reassuring them that everyone will be fine and taken care of at all times.
- Celebrate their lives.

- Tell your loved one out loud or in your heart that you love them and just what they mean to you.
- Allow the room to be quiet when needed, too much activity is not good for anyone involved.

Fifth Level of Transition

5th Dimension of Light / Throat Chakra / Auric Etheric Template

Shuts down the consciousness of *"all we experience"* as the *BODY* of Universe Energies

Fifth Level Summary

- The dying person can be directly unresponsive and/or can flip flop from conscious to unconscious.
- There is a letting go of all individual consciousness.
- They harmoniously merge back to a collective consciousness.
- Their eyes are sometimes opening and searching.
- Spirit-helpers begin to arrive to assist the person.
- There may be talking, looking, or reaching at someone in the room that is not there to our physical eyes.
- Breathing stops only to start up again.

What I *Psychically See* at this Level

During this time, I psychically *see* beautiful etheric beings beginning to come into the person's room. At this time, these beings usually are staying around the perimeter of the room, hovering in the corners.

Psychically, I also begin to see heavenly white light of Source dimly beginning to align from the far corner of the dying person's room. This directly corresponds to the path of the vertical lines of energy that represent the person's chakras still working to dissolve.

As I work to assist the person through this phase, their throat chakra is now seen as a vertical line. It will go dark and then dissolve, moving the entire pathway closer to the light. I also can now begin to see them communicate with the spiritual helpers in the room, as they reach out and whisper in communication to them. I can sometimes hear them communicating with their guides and helpers, because at this point we no longer need our human voice.

By now, I usually am aware of their personal Guardian Angel, oftentimes standing at the left shoulder of the person.

As they continue to release their fifth dimension of light and throat chakra, their etheric template of the aura dissolves. It is a transmuting of energy—a returning to Source.

What Your Loved One *May Be* Psychically Experiencing at this Level

Because this is the communication chakra, the dying person remembers their knowing of telepathic conversing, and this offers a new sense of joyous return to family. Your loved one's Higher Self begins to take the lead in connecting with the incoming energies of love and support from guides, angels, and loved ones who begin to manifest with more detail. This is why we see the dying person act as if they are speaking with someone who we think isn't necessarily there, but indeed they are—from an energetic perspective. This connection may be strong or weak, depending on the belief system of the person.

For me, this fifth level of transition also offers the initial awareness of the white light and the path towards it. Many people find themselves in awe during this phase and may make verbal reference to it.

Healing Strategies for this Level

- Make sure you and all caregivers are getting sufficient rest, food, and fresh air.
- If the time is appropriate, begin to allow your loved one to go, to move onward, and let them return to Source. Oftentimes they need our permission.
- If this is the case, tell them that all those who are left behind will be just fine and reassure the person that all things will be taken care of for them.

- Begin to let go yourself and try not to control the situation. Honor the journey and the soul contract of your loved one.
- Express your thoughts and feelings with your loved one, either out loud or in your heart.

Sixth Level of Transition

6th Dimension of Light / The Third-Eye Chakra or Brow / Auric Celestial Body

Final Release of *"all we create"* as the *MIND* of Universe Energies

Sixth Level Summary

- Releasing language of life, light, and the knowledge of form and structure.
- There may be a soft glow emanating from the dying person's face and body.

What I *Psychically See* at this Level

During this time, I psychically *see* the entire room and surroundings take on an opaque or pearly-soft look. I also see the white light actually begin to make itself known in the upper corner of the room. The spiritual helpers gain in vibration and, energetically, begin to move closer to the side of the bed or surround the person. They place themselves at the head and foot of the bed, eventually filling in all the sides. I see them as gold and white light beings. I also can sense who they are and what they have to say, so I work to assist the person through this phase of communication. Their third-eye chakra, now seen as one of the last vertical lines, will go dark and then dissolve, moving the entire pathway even closer to the light.

This usually is a fast-paced phase, as they continue to release their sixth dimension of light and third-eye chakra to dissolve their celestial body of the aura. It is a transmuting of energy—a returning to Source.

What Your Loved One *May Be* Psychically Experiencing at this Level

The dying person's psychic self has fully kicked in at the sixth level as they now intuitively embrace their truth of returning home and aligning with Source or God. They also have full awareness of the benevolent help that surrounds them and know that they can call upon more helpers if they choose.

As the person becomes more aware, their co-creation moves into high gear to forge their path back home and the white light now becomes more defined. When the person begins energetically to enter the white light that holds their Akashic Record, this is what we might recognize as the feeling or sensation of moving through a tunnel back to Source. From a psychic standpoint, this tunnel is the etheric silver cord or tentacle of energy that connects the human incarnation to the soul-self from conception through final death. The consciousness is now working in a curious, calm, mindful state of bliss-filled surrender.

Healing Strategies for this Level

- Make sure you and all caregivers are getting sufficient rest, food, and fresh air.
- Continue to let go yourself and try not to control the situation. Honor the journey and the soul contract of your loved one.
- Try your best to allow yourself some quality meditative time with your loved one and the room itself to see if you can connect to the guidance entering at this stage.
- Allow yourself to fully grieve but also try your best to find gratitude for participating in this process.
- Pray, sing, spend these last hours in the manner your loved one would appreciate.
- Express your thoughts and feelings with your loved one, either out loud or in your heart.

Seventh Level of Transition

7th Dimension of Light / Crown Chakra / Auric Ketheric Template
Final Release of *"all we experience"* as the *BODY* of Celestial Soul Energies

Seventh Level Summary

- Now releases *ALL* shape and form.
- Releases all harmonics of creation itself.
- The dying person moves from the sixth level quickly and uneventfully through the seventh level.

What I *Psychically See* at this Level

During this time, I psychically *see* the spirit-helpers grow even stronger now in vibration as their glow of bright yellow, gold, and white light becomes more vibrant and more unified. The frequency of the energy within the room amplifies.

As I work to assist the person through this phase, their crown chakra, now seen as the very last vertical line, will be the last to go dark and then dissolve, moving the entire pathway closer to the light.

Psychically I continue to see the white light merge closer with the person. As they continue to release, their seventh dimension/crown chakra of light dissolves their ketheric template of the aura. It is a transmuting of energy—a returning to Source.

What Your Loved One *May Be* Psychically Experiencing at this Level

Even though the physical human body is still in transition, the psychic energetic body traversus further into the tunnel to examine the properties of their Akashic Record, either to fully surrender to the return of Source, or not. In a near death experience (NDE), this is when the person chooses to return to their human body reality, most likely because they examined their Record and determined they still have work to do. Those in alignment with the "Return to Source" energetic file will continue onward through the tunnel.

Healing Strategies for this Level

- Make sure you and all caregivers are getting sufficient rest, food, and fresh air.
- Continual gratitude is key now, being grateful for this experience of transition.
- Try to keep the situation reverent as the journey is coming to an end soon.
- Continue to journal all experiences as you will cherish these moments in months and years to come.
- Express your thoughts and feelings with your loved one, either out loud or in your heart.

Eighth Level of Transition

Final Release of *"all we create"* as the *MIND* of Celestial Soul Energies

Eighth Level Summary

- Physical body of the person has most likely taken its last human breath.
- Spirit is still at work to move to and through the next level.
- Next levels of movement are combined and very quick.

What I *Psychically See* at this Level

During this time, I psychically *see* the continuation of the Spirit-helpers working and the white light merging closer with the person. It is a transmuting of energy—a returning to Source.

What Your Loved One *May Be* Psychically Experiencing at this Level

Now the human body has expired from a 3-D standpoint, but the person's energy body and spirit guides are still at work. The person is now deep into their white-light tunnel psychic experience and has fully surrendered to aligning with Source. The guides, loved ones, angels, and benevolent beings will also now merge into the white-light tunnel to accompany the person. The white light continues to expand until it fully transmutes all energies into one, while at the same time, fills the person's room with love-light energy for anyone in attendance.

During this stage, the omnipresence of the transmuting soul is now fully able to connect with whomever he or she chooses in any time/space continuum. This is why so many have a sense of the time and date a loved one dies, even from afar.

Healing Strategies for this Level

- This is probably the most difficult stage to concentrate on any sense of awe or wonder, as the person has most likely just taken their last physical breath and is now what we would call clinically dead. Most holding vigil are so emotionally frightened, sad, or angry, that they understandably miss the opportunity to see Spirit at work during this phase. Sometimes, at a later time, we can recount the experience and many spiritual moments can be remembered.
- Yes, tears and emotions are a normal part of this phase, so honor what it is that your body needs to do to experience this without judgment of self or others.
- Stay in the room, leave the room, or go back and forth— find what works for you during this time as your loved one is still transitioning aurically and throughout the room.
- Do not rush this time. Be patient with your grief, allowing yourself time and space.

Ninth Level of Transition

Final Release of *"all we create"* and experience as the *MIND* and the *BODY*

Ninth Level Summary

- The person is "gone," but Spirit is still in transition.
- Now working in infinite love and light residing in all dimensions.
- All vertical veils of the dimensions now fade.

- The person is in the state of "crossing over" into the white light.

What I *Psychically See* at this Level

During this time, I psychically *see* the final stages of the Spirit-helpers and the white light fully merging with the person. It is the final steps of the transmuting of human energy fully returning to Source energy.

I also can feel the celestial soul energy of the person moving into the light, and crossing over into the light feels somewhat like a very slight and subtle sensation of an up and over movement. It is a smooth but distinct knowing they moved beyond the veil. My own physical body sometimes is overwhelmed with an incredible sensation of love that causes me to shed tears of joy. It is an honor to be allowed to witness this miracle of transmutation back to Source.

Edgar Cayce's *Origin and Destiny of Man* states: "All souls were created in the beginning, and are finding their way back to whence they came." I believe wholeheartedly in this statement. I believe we all can draw strength from these wise words as we assist a loved one along their journey back to spirit.

What Your Loved One *May Be* Psychically Experiencing at this Level

During the Ninth Level, the transition continues, as does the transmutation into the field of omnipresence while the soul multi-tasks existing on both sides of the veil simultaneously. The living may (or may not) distinctly experience the feeling of their loved one's presence directly following their death around the home, during their funeral, or at any services.

When that supportive presence seems to dissipate or become non-existent (or, if you did not feel it at all) those of us in the physical world can become fear-filled because we believe we have lost connection to our newly passed loved one. The transitioning spirit-body is "busy" attending to the terms and review of the Akashic Record of their completed incarnation. It's important for us to remember that they are always there for us, but the degree of the connection can fluctuate. Patience is key.

Healing Strategies for this Level

- If you are present with your loved one at the last moments of their life, try your best to honor the space within the room following their passing. Sit in quiet reverence if at all possible because the level of spirit is intense and can assist you in finding peace in the transition.
- You may want to write about your experience, journaling about your loved one. Acknowledge what you have been through in the experience from your perspective.
- Do not rush this time. Be patient with your grief, allowing yourself time and space.
- Continue to share stories.
- Continue to be grateful for being allowed to witness the experience.
- If you were not able to be present, you can also feel and know all the same experiences from afar. Remember, our loved ones oftentimes make a goodbye visit when they choose to transition, so look for the signs and be grateful.

Acknowledgments

I would like to wholeheartedly thank the many hospice patients who assisted me in understanding the stages of the death process. I could not have done this work without their input, which they offered unconditionally with loving energy. In addition to the patients, I would like to acknowledge the staff of hospice. I would like to especially thank my Volunteer Coordinators, Renee and Ruth, without whom this book would not have been written. Their encouragement, leadership, and hearts went well beyond their job descriptions.

A word of gratitude to my many clients who have allowed me the opportunity to learn through their energy healing experiences. Their love and openness has assisted me in honing my metaphysical skills and expanding any God-given gifts.

To my family and friends who have supported me through these past couple of years as I searched for balance and focus. To my parents without whom my belief system would not have been rooted. To my husband Chuck who is my grounding, my rock. And to my four children: Ryan, Blake, Mitchell, and Phoebe, whose ongoing patience and encouragement continues to allow me the time and space to create.

I would like to thank my metaphysical mentors, friends, and my own personal guides, angels, and light people who have guided me along this journey. They have energetically continued to offer downloads of information that would not have been available to me through traditional channels of learning.

I would like to thank Kelsey and her true gift of words that continually assisted me in taking my concepts forward. Her ability to formulate concise edits were so valuable to present this information in a clear and user-friendly manner. And to Annie for the technical and emotional support of this project, and for making this information available to all those who deserve to learn from it. And Tracie, for her sharp eye, attention to detail, and pristine sense of grammar—all of which offered the final clarity for this project to launch!

And probably most importantly, I am forever thankful to my friend Rick, who through his death process taught me to see from the perspective of my heart rather than my head.

From all of you that support me, I have *learned* … so now I can *teach*.

Note

I would like to acknowledge with gratitude the following authors whose work has influenced this book:

Rev. Dr. David Laurance Bieniek, *At the Time of Death: Symbols & Rituals for Caregivers & Chaplains* (Berkeley, CA: Apocryphile Press, 2019).

Barbara Brennan, *Hands of Light* (New York: Bantam Books/ Random House Publishing, 1988).

Christopher Penczak, *Ascension Magick: Ritual, Myth & Healing for the New Aeon* (Woodbury, MN: Llewellyn Publications, 2007).

About the Author

Photo by Nicolle Danús

Suzanne Worthley is an energy healing practitioner and intuitive who has studied and worked professionally in the field for nearly two decades. She offers personal healings, space healings, spirit work, crossing over work, clearing work, and vigil/death and dying work. Suzanne has played a vital role in partnership with families and hospice teams for nearly a decade, helping the dying have a peaceful transition, and helping families and caregivers understand what is happening energetically during the death process.

Suzanne's work includes teaching individuals and groups and counseling clients on the subjects of energy, healing, personal power, protection, and the Higher Self. She hosts many metaphysical and healing events, including spiritual tours of Peru, and offers webinars, meditations, workshops, products on consciousness studies and energy. She has a monthly membership-based online community, *Vibe Tribe*, that offers ongoing training and forums for learning, discussion, and support.

Visit Suzanne online at **www.sworthley.com.**

FINDHORN PRESS

Life-Changing Books

Consult our catalogue online
(with secure order facility) on
www.findhornpress.com

For information on the Findhorn Foundation:
www.findhorn.org